The Sloane Rover's Handbook

THE Sloane Rover's HANDBOOK

Francesca Findlater

Illustrations by Anthony Grant

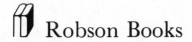 Robson Books

First published in United Kingdom in 1985 by
Robson Books Ltd., Bolsover House, 5-6 Clipstone Street,
London W1P 7EB. Copyright © Francesca Findlater
1985.

Designed by Anne Davison

British Library Cataloguing in Publication Data

Findlater, Francesca
   The Sloane Rover's handbook.
   1. Title
   828'.91407   PN6175

ISBN 0-86051-349-1

Printed in the United Kingdom by St Edmundsbury Press,
Bury St Edmunds, Suffolk.

Contents

Thank you

David, China, Cushion, Bogart, Mel, Rod and Francis

Introduction

How to recognise a Sloane Rover is undoubtedly the question uppermost in all our minds. Until now the elusiveness of the answer has caused sleepless nights and feelings of great personal inadequacy, but no longer — this Handbook tries to pinpoint the Essence of Sloane Roverdom for the uninitiated. To assist immediate streetwise recognition, and to satisfy the initial burning need for more information, listed below are a few primary pointers:

- The Sloane Rover prefers to ride in a Range Rover.
- The Sloane Rover coordinates very well indeed with Osborne and Little wallpaper.
- The Sloane Rover will not go into a garden with crazy paving.
- Sloane Rovers understand the importance of royalty.
- Sloane Rovers love going shooting, to point-to-points, Badminton, Ascot and Henley.
- Sloane Rovers recognise the importance of the Barbour and the Husky, and may occasionally wear one themselves.
- Sloane Rovers learn young to go after breakfast, never say die, never show off and never whine.
- Sloane Rovers know which way to pass the port.

This book was largely researched by a London Sloane Rover called China. She has first-hand knowledge of the capital and of a number of particularly Sloane outposts in other parts of England, as well as being in correspondence with well-travelled Basset cousins who live in the South of France, for whose recommendations she is particularly grateful. China would also like to thank friends from other countries who have recommended their favourite spots and contributed sections on their own countries. In addition, she has talked to that well-known Top Dog, C. M. McMuck of Bucklesham Hall, and his comments are included in a number of chapters.

1 *Acquiring the Sloane Rover*

The decision to acquire a Sloane Rover (or Sloane Dog, as we shall call it to avoid any possible confusion) is undoubtedly one of the most important that the Sloane Dog Owner will ever make. The process is not unlike that of deciding to marry, and requires the same elements of careful consideration and luck. The element of luck may be reduced by due consideration of the following salient points:

Breeding This means the kind of family names that can be dropped during dinner party conversation and make the rest of the guests extremely jealous. (Alternatively, if not well bred — and even a mongrel has the potential to be a Sloane Dog — then the dog must be full of personality and have scandalously misplaced breeding. E.g., 'Ch. Perfectnose of Bighouseincountry got out, and guess who she met in the kitchen garden?')

Compatibility Compromise is not a strong feature of the Sloane Dog so a degree of compatibility is essential. Such characteristics as laziness, fitness, ambition, eccentricity (is he or she a snappy dresser?), sociability (is it a cocktail party

SD or just a country house party SD? Does it enjoy dinner parties or just rock concerts?) must be given due attention. They are all highly relevant.

It should also be noted that the SD deviates slightly from accepted Sloane behaviour and tends to get involved in things that would make the average Sloane Ranger shiver in her Barbour. For example, the odd eyebrow might well be raised if the typical SDO (Sloane Dog Owner) were to enter the Miss World competition, but a champion SD at Crufts is much prized as a thing of wonderment and beauty and a mark of great success. Thus the Sloane Dog has more scope for eccentric activities than its owner.

Once the decision to acquire a lifelong companion has been made, the next major drama is rather like choosing an article of clothing — which breed will suit me? Inevitably the potential SDO does not have a choice from every breed there is, for he has to choose a suitably Sloane breed. The next few pages, therefore, give a brief guide to the currently acceptable face of Sloane Dog Ownership.

Is it lively? ... Is it lazy?

The current top twenty breeds of dog are: German Shepherd, Yorkshire Terrier, Labrador, Golden Retriever, Cavalier King Charles Spaniel, Cocker Spaniel, Springer Spaniel, Rough Collie, Doberman, Shetland Sheepdog, Boxer, Old English Sheepdog, Toy Poodle, West Highland White Terrier, Staffordshire Bull Terrier, Irish Setter, Pekingese, Cairn Terrier, Great Dane, Long-coated Chihuahua.

Of these breeds, some are naturally more Sloane than others, and other Sloane favourites should be included such as the Dachshund, Sealyham, Jack Russell, Lurcher, and, through its royal connections, the Corgi. One or two other breeds which we have not gone into in depth — such as Shi Tzus and Lhaso Apsos — are also now creeping up the popularity charts, revealing a trend towards the 'moving rug' type of breed. We have outlined a few crucial characteristics of the different breeds below:

Labrador Black or golden — the ultimate SD. Needs a lot of exercise, loves the country life (beware the early chewing phase). Adores the SDO's ratlet (child). The golden version goes very well with classic green-dominated chintzes — looks terrific against the curtains. The black colour-way blends well with everything, particularly the dark.

Retriever See Labrador and add hair.

Yorkshire Terrier Makes up in character what it lacks in size — a jolly little SD ideal for carrying in a basket, preferably a Louis Vuitton Dog Carrying Basket, but also an ordinary shoulder basket or a bicycle basket. Not really an SDO chap's dog, but nonetheless a perky little thing. Don't be fooled by its short little legs, it's more than capable of going the distance.

German Shepherd Butch in appearance, butch by nature. Needs a pretty serious SDO to get the best from it and exercise and train it properly (otherwise there is a strong possibility it may turn on and devour its SDO). Not suitable for the faint-hearted.

Cavalier King Charles Spaniel An extremely cheerful little SD with royal connections far back into its past. Royal decrees all over the place. Saves on china ornaments in the house — two of these negate the need for the Staffordshires on the mantelpiece. Ideal SD for the foodie — eats like a maniac.

Cocker Spaniel The next model up with equally cheerful disposition. Bred as a game dog which makes it highly acceptable, although it doesn't look as good on the mantelpiece.

English Springer Spaniel The largest model in the trio. Bright(ish) and a good gun dog and pet — which is pretty much all any SDO could want. Needs plenty of exercise or tends to get fat, which does rather spoil the image. Goes superbly with a mahogany and cream silk colour scheme.

Rough Collie Lassie was the prime example so it's a bit like having son of Superman in your house — you always expect it to save you, clean the house, be a nanny, pay the milkman and remember birthdays. Don't. These dogs prefer the country, and may occasionally need vacuum cleaning.

Doberman Another statement of strength and excellent for protecting the family heirlooms, although can be surprisingly soppy at times. Needs lots of walks. It is strongly recommended that you do not spring a surprise on this particular SD in the middle of the night — you might well not live to regret it.

Boxer Tends towards fragility owing to inherited facial characteristics. Very much the chinless wonder of the SD world, the Boxer is not suitable for the marathon runner who likes a trot in the hot sunshine, because its shortened face may cause breathing difficulties, and stress may lead to fainting. Thus the Boxer comes with its own built-in excuse for not exercising.

Old English Sheepdog A dream with baby SDOs and excellent for resting your feet on. Hell to groom, but not bad on exercise — not wild about long walks. Happy to potter about in the garden, but there must be a garden.

Toy Poodle Not very Sloane, but a delightful, organized character who expects meals, walks and ball-playing absolutely on schedule. Main advantage is that it doesn't shed hair. Exhibits French bourgeois characteristics which is possibly why the streets of France are practically paved with (and by) them!

West Highland White Terrier No colour scheme problems, white goes well with everything. Hardy enough to overcome his size. Bred as a fox hunter which could come in useful. Good Scottish connections.

Staffordshire Bull Terrier Advisable to keep this one on a lead when it's out and about because despite enormous loyalty to its SDO it's a bit of a pub brawler and tends to look for fights. Not frightfully Sloane.

Irish Setter Delightful good looks, but a charming, absent-minded lack of discipline means that the Irish Setter is no good as a guard dog despite its size. Excellent colouring, however, looks wonderful against pink, coral and crimson, if slightly over the top.

Pekingese Another royal dog, this one's image is not very dynamic, and it tends towards a spoilt nature. Trots happily on reasonable walks but may ask for a lift half-way — be prepared. Reasonably good for the sedentary SDO.

Cairn Terrier Has been a royal favourite in its time — an energetic chap who definitely needs a garden and long walks. Boisterous and suitably social.

Great Dane Terrific for the SDO's image, giving the impression of massive wealth, and not bad on exercise either — happy to live in a flat. The reason it indicates great wealth, of course, is that it eats a butcher's shop full of meat per week. It is also a tricky one if you're not good at discipline — it can do a remarkable amount of damage to both people and country houses in a very short time, not to mention the fact that one piddle on the carpet and the house is under water.

Long-Coated Chihuahua The other end of the scale, but ideal as a go-anywhere companion providing great care is taken at all times not to sit on it. Extremely suitable for the older SDO as it requires little exercise and little food — although it tends to be a faddy foodie. Loves the perfect-sized portions of the *nouvelle cuisine*.

Pembroke Welsh Corgi Due to its royal connections, a very SD. Slight tendency to bite (which can, of course, be used to advantage). Prefers typically SD country life with plenty of exercise, or can get unfashionably podgy.

Jack Russell Not just SD, positively Hooray, tends to hurl itself about with appalling abandon. Excessively perky, sporty, handy-sized without being twee, excitable and (here's the rub) not actually accepted by the Kennel Club as a breed. This makes very little difference because it is nonetheless a popular Sloane breed.

Sealyham Terrier Another SD that has graced the royal gardens in its time. An attractive SD with a lovely long white coat. Naturally its greatest love is to get extremely dirty. Another perky little charmer whose only disadvantage may be its hairdressing bills.

Dachshund The Dachshund has built up a great strength of character — it has had to, for not only does its tummy practically touch the ground, which must take a bit of getting used to, but during one period in its history it was stoned for its strong German association. There is a variety to choose from — smooth-haired, long-haired or wire-haired — and it is always good to have a choice. Possible drawback — or maybe an advantage — is that it has a loud bark and a tendency to attack strange ankles.

The Mélange The SD of dubious parentage but overwhelming charm, intelligence, style and, of course, colour co-ordination (possibility of so many colours it will go with every room in the house).

Once the commitment has been made, the model selected, and the mortgage taken out in preparation, the next question must be 'What star sign should I choose for total compatibility?'. The following brief run-down of canine star signs is offered as a guideline.

THE STARS

ARIES March 21–April 20

A pioneering beast, always at the forefront, thus might pull on his lead. Enthusiastic, but also impulsive, self-willed, independent and headstrong — so training could be laborious. Enormous amounts of energy — often too much, and tendency to impatience.
Keynote: Assertive.
Physical appearance: Tends towards lean and wiry, often goes grey early in life.
Compatible signs: Exuberance well controlled by Virgo or Capricorn. Whirled into excitement by Sagittarius and Leo, and calmed by Libra.

TAURUS April 21–May 21

Reserved, patient, and diplomatic — but stubborn and solid — so will dig his paws in and end up getting dragged across a muddy path. Excellently suited to the diplomatic life — calm and dignified. Faithful and warm-hearted in its attachments, and self-controlled, but pushed beyond normal limits will go bananas. Loves luxury, and very fixed in likes and dislikes.

Keynote: Determination.

Physical appearance: Short and solid, looks hard to rouse.

Compatible signs: Not the unconventional types — Aquarius or Sagittarius couldn't cope. Best with Virgo, Capricorn or Scorpio to cater for love of luxury.

GEMINI May 22–June 21

Artistic by nature — but lacking in concentration. Loves walking, and writing — many dog authors are Gemini. Loves a lot of movement and change. Quick-witted so learns fast, although slightly nervous and restless. Loves the limelight.

Keynote: Versatility.

Physical appearance: Slim, neat paws, hair tends to thin with age.

Compatible signs: Sagittarius offers intellectual stimulation; Libra and Aquarius would enjoy the same interests; but not Scorpio or Taurus, they're too demanding.

CANCER June 22–July 23

Sympathetic and sensitive but with emotional tendencies. Slightly shy and reserved, but also loves publicity which means it could be a potential flasher — watch for tell-tale signs. Easily influenced — so might leave home, especially as very adaptable. Contradictorily cautious by nature and often with psychic tendencies. Loves the seaside, the home and the family.

Keynote: Tenacity.

Physical appearance: Average to small, tendency towards fleshiness.

Compatible signs: Scorpio, Taurus or Capricorn good for providing security. Livened up by Pisces, but not Aries, Sagittarius or Leo — all too fiery.

LEO July 24–August 23

Ambitious and aspiring with tendency to take control — lethal in a Great Dane. Nonetheless exhibits responsibility and often has a magnetic personality, very sociable and pleasure-loving and full of self-confidence. Has strong and

deep feelings — so must be treated with respect and not hurt. A perfectionist — likes his kennel just so.
Keynote: Affection.
Physical appearance: Largish build — and often with curly hair.
Compatible signs: Not Virgo, Capricorn or Taurus (too boring). Sagittarius, Aries, or Aquarius all have the same zest for life and social contacts.

VIRGO August 24–September 23

Practical, analytical and discriminating — so won't do anything it thinks is unreasonable. Excellent mental abilities — so can be trained for acting or police work. Prefers to work with another dog to bring out the best, as slightly lacking in confidence. Can be rather reserved, and the weak points are selfishness and arrogance — won't share his *Daube* of Chum. Tend to be faddy about food, and very fussy about dress. Also a hypochondriac.
Keynote: Discrimination.
Physical appearance: Well-proportioned, ages well, sometimes pigeon-toed.
Compatible signs: Capricorn and Pisces give the warmth needed, but not Aries, Gemini or Sagittarius — too demanding.

LIBRA September 24–October 23

Refined by nature, loves pleasure, cheerful disposition — good tail-wagger and very sociable. Affectionate and romantic so will appreciate those candle-lit dinners at home. Slightly impatient, but very persistent. Idealistic and needs a harmonious home — not suitable for families in which divorce is impending.
Keynote: Balance.
Physical appearance: Excellent cruising material, as often have superb bodies, although inclined to stoutness in old age.
Compatible signs: Popular with most signs. Gemini and Aquarius good to keep Librans on their toes.

SCORPIO October 24–November 22

Firm, determined and obstinate. Full of energy, proud and self-confident. Loves delving into the secrets of nature — i.e.

digging up the garden. Has a forceful temperament and a tendency to rampant sexuality.
Keynote: Enthusiasm.
Physical appearance: Muscular and strong. Often very hairy.
Compatible signs: Cancer or Pisces can share enthusiasm, Taurus for the good things in life but not Aquarius or Leo — too bossy.

SAGITTARIUS November 23–December 22

Active, enterprising and independent. Loves freedom and has an inclination to be slightly brazen, might well have to be retrieved from the dog pound. Loves exercise and the great outdoors. Zealous and courageous. An excellent police dog.
Keynote: Aspiration.
Physical appearance: Wiry, loose-limbed, large paws.
Compatible signs: Not Scorpio or Taurus. Aries or Leo are good matches and Gemini for mental compatibility.

CAPRICORN December 23–January 20

Persevering, so good to train; ambitious and responsible. Desirous of power and fame so excellent for brave deeds. Trustworthy and reliable, but not very demonstrative.
Keynote: Stability.
Physical appearance: Average to small stature, bony and prone to dry skin.
Compatible signs: Virgo, Taurus or another Capricorn. Cancer is also a possibility.

AQUARIUS January 21–February 19

Shy and retiring nature but very intuitive. Needs harmonious surroundings. Constant in affection and loves children. Quiet and unassuming. Unfortunately tends to like strangers.
Keynote: Universal love of mankind.
Physical appearance: Tall, erect, dignified.
Compatible signs: Gemini, Sagittarius or Libra are best suited; Leo sometimes.

PISCES February 20–March 20

Sensitive, sympathetic, receptive to ideas, impressionable but

not demonstrative. Slightly wet-natured — doesn't fight
back and tends to be put upon. Can be slightly boring, but
very dependable.
Keynote: Service.
Physical appearance: Tendency to fat — fleshy and soft.
Compatible signs: Cancer, Scorpio or Virgo.

At last the brief is complete and the next step is nigh. A
question looms: 'Where do I go to get my Sloane Dog?' The
immediate and flippant answer is, of course, a pet shop, but
this begs a whole series of questions. If a pet shop, then
which pet shop? If not a pet shop, then where? A breeder?
Which breeder? If not a breeder, then whom? Whom can I
ask, where do I find these Sloane Doggy people? Might my
potential SD be advertised in any publication? Is there a
Debrett's in which to check its pedigree? In other words —
panic.

The answer to the pet shop is simple. Without wishing to
cut corners: Harrods. They are helpful, friendly and *au fait*
with the SDO's requirement, and in any case it's far quicker
and easier to go straight to the Sloane nucleus. Naturally, if
London is too far to travel, then one of the options will have
to be taken up.

In America two years ago the famous Nieman Marcus
Christmas catalogue was offering His and Hers Shar Pei
puppies for sale for £2,000, but this is not really suggested as
a serious option. Plucking the potential SD from the bosom
of its family where you can see it in its natural environment
and determine its true background is to be highly
recommended. To find a breeder it is best to contact the
Debrett's of the dog world, the Kennel Club, and ask for a
list of breeders of the particular model you are seeking.
Selection is often largely decided by the litters available and
their proximity. For sensible advice there is always the
National Dog Owners' Association, who will be happy to
help differentiate between Sloane and non-Sloane. You will
find Sloane Dogs advertised in *The Times* and magazine like
Country Life and *Horse and Hound*. Alternatively, you may
prefer to seek advice by loitering at point-to-points or asking
your friends. Both alternatives are fairly good bets.

The Mélange is a somewhat different matter, and may
well come from a number of diverse sources — a friend of a

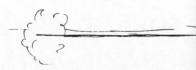

friend, perhaps, or it may even be waiting in Battersea Dogs' Home for the SDO with a social conscience to come and rescue it (particularly acceptable now that Battersea is so much more 'OK'). There are many organisations that care for unwanted animals including the excellent National Canine Defence League who pride themselves on the fact that no healthy dog is ever put down, however old, and who completely rehabilitate all the dogs they find. The main advantage of Battersea Dogs' Home is that it is convenient, and everyone has heard of it. If they are prepared to endure the emotional problems but still want the looks, fussier SDOs with a social conscience can choose the kind of dog they want and then contact the Rescue Society of that particular breed.

Whatever source you get it from, and however much (or little) investment you put into acquiring it, once the SD is in its new home, the fun has only just begun...

Some suitably Sloane pet shops
Animal Fair, 17 Abingdon Road, W8
Town and Country Dogs, 35b Sloane Street, SW1
Kensington Dog Bureau, 3a Kensington Church Walk, W8.

Useful addresses
Battersea Dogs' Home, 4 Battersea Park Road, SW8
National Canine Defence League, 1 & 2 Pratt Mews, NW1.

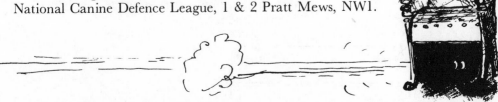

2 *Naming the Sloane Rover*

Trying to find the perfect name is a task second only to that of acquiring the noble hound. It is very important for the SDO to be able to shout a suitable name across royal parks, London streets, country lanes and through the corridors of numerous Sloane residences throughout the country, so the name does not just reflect on the SD, it positively shines on the SDO — and speaks volumes about him or her.

Enquiries among some registration organisations have produced the following list of the most popular names, which vary considerably in their Sloane-ness — a few (particularly the girls' names) are really quite acceptable, but some SDOs might prefer something slight more original: *Snoopy, Dougal, Lucky, Bonzo, Shep, Ben, Sam, Brandy, Whisky, Patch, Butch, Rover, Skipper, Prince, Rex, Lassie, Sophie, Emma, Tessa, Zöe.*

Naturally, there is also the kennel name: *Ch. Elch Elder of Ouborough, Ch. Tzigane Aggri of Nashend, Ch. Hendrawen's Nibelung of Charavigne,* and such like, but these are not normally in everyday use.

As with children it is worth considering the initials when naming the SD — do they go well with the surname? Will they look good monogrammed on the towels, linen, etc? And will it sound too silly at the christening?

A few suggestions for names follow, divided into useful categories:

a) The simple, easy to remember/easy to call/unpretentious.

Happy	King George V had a dog called Happy who wrote a book called *If I Were King George.*
Dookie	The name given to the first royal Corgi.
Spott	Notice the double 't' — which adds a touch of Sloane to an otherwise dull name.
Phideaux	Note the spelling — the equivalent of Higginbothom.

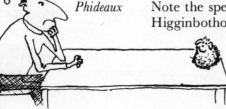

Down Boy	Obviously relates to the behaviour of the SD you have acquired. Since this command is always on your lips, the dog now responds as though it were its name.
Blackié	Notice the accent on the 'e', which adds a certain style. An obvious name, but better if the SD is white.
Phred	Another attempt to liven up an otherwise very uninspired name.
Henry	Definitely SD.
Caroline	Equally so.
Grub	Not an attractive name but succinct. Ideal for the aspiring foodie.
Mally	A name chosen by one SDO who was building a trout farm when her Springer Spaniel puppy fell into a pot of malachite. The name stuck (so did the malachite).

b) The name that's full of originality, character and humour — revealing chapters about SD and SDO.

Butch	Slightly obvious, but requires little explanation.
Divine	Again, lacking in subtlety but catchy.
Tatler	Sums up a chatty little beast — can extend to Vogue and Harpers and Ritz.
Sexy	Disgustingly obvious but could prove extremely amusing in the park.

Battersea	Witty, and opens up a gamut of names — Chelsea, Clapham, Mayfair, Belgravia.
Humphrey	Distinctive, if a little pompous.
Paris	City and country names lend themselves well — London, New York, Japan (Yugoslavia and Czechoslovakia are not so catchy, but the simple ones are quite stylish).
Champagne	Names that indicate a personal passion are interesting — e.g. caviare, toast, Marmite, music, drugs (cannabis is better).
Truffle	A foodie favourite.
Harrods	Why not? Also Fortnums, Simpsons, etc., etc.

c) The name that honours a personal hero/heroine.

Hattie	The heroic mongrel who survived the Libyan siege. Honeybun was also a hero, but he was a rabbit.
Joan	Lends itself well to a bitch, others on the same lines include Raquel, Krystal, Fallon, Pamela, Sue Ellen.
JR	Could encourage more violence than is really necessary? Perhaps Bobby, Clayton, Cliff, Carrington and Colby are other possibilities.
Bert	Burt Reynolds may be a hero, but would this really do him justice?
Mountbatten	An excellent tribute, but one that could only be awarded to a very worthy dog.
Westminster	Very suitable, if slightly similar to Battersea.
Diana	This leads on to all the members of the Royal Family but without their prefixes the names lose some of their ring, and it is difficult to shout two names all the time (Andrew, Anne, Alexandra, Helen, Michael, Charles).
Carrier	Costa, Grigson, etc, for the foodie hero.
Margaret	Or Thatcher — the latter is probably catchier.
Jagger	And, of course, myriads of others on the same lines — one envisages endless SDs running around called Wham, Roxy Music, Duran, etc. — slightly over the top.
Hollywood	An excellent generalisation.

d) The historical name — often with a story attached —
    excellent when someone asks how your SD got its name
    (they'll wish they had never asked).

Anubis	The dog-headed god, you can't get much more ambitious than that.
Baskerville	Could be a good name for a hound.
Norfolk	County names enter here as strongly Shakespearian-sounding — Pembroke, Buckingham, Bolingbroke, etc.
Boadicea	An SDO popular heroine — a bit of a mouthful, however.
Arthur	King Arthur, not Arthur Scargill — could be confusing.
Carpaccio	A well-known dog lover who put them in all his paintings — leads on to Veronese, the best-known dog lover in Italian art, and to Titian. (Gainsborough also loved dogs, particularly Pomeranians.)
Briso	The name of Rosa Bonheur's sheepdog.
Trump	Hogarth's dog's name.
Capone	A bit more down to earth — folk hero rather than historical — leads into quite lively names such as Legs and Bugsy.
Rabelais	And other literary heroes — Sartre, Dickens, Cocteau.
Escoffier	For the historical foodie — or Boulestin, Carême, etc.
Argus	An excellent talking point — the ultimate faithful hound: 'There, full of vermin, lay Argus, the hound. But directly he became aware of Odysseus's presence he wagged his tail and dropped his ears...'
Burgundy	The Duke had 1,500 dogs — a keen SDO.
Bosun'	Byron's dog.

e) The same as that of a celebrity's — something
    to aspire to.

Bobo Buckinghamshire	(Lady Buckinghamshire)
Alphonse	(The Duchess of Argyll)
Gigot	(Mary Quant)

Tara, Honey, Liebschen, Bindy and *Nina*	(Bea Nash)
JoJo and *Busy Lizzie*	(Katie Boyle)
Bob	(Peter Bowles)
Orme	(Jill Bennett)
Spotty Boy	(Lord Chancellor Hailsham)
Spot and *Snoopy*	(Sally Oppenheim)

THE CHRISTENING

Once the name is selected, the christening looms ahead. This is not so much a name-giving ceremony as an excuse for a glass of champagne and the giving of presents. It is also a very good opportunity to appoint a 'godparent', who rather than undertaking the religious education of his or her ward, undertakes a holiday sitting and is supportive in case of problems.

Suitable christening presents are really essentials that every Sloane Dog worthy of the name needs on a day-to-day basis — a case of champagne (quarter bottles), and engraved silver tin-opener or an engraved silver dog bowl, or possibly a monogrammed Atkinson cashmere blanket (£600) from Harrods, which will last for the SD's life and stand him in excellent stead. If any of these items do not appear as presents they will have to be purchased anyway, so encourage your friends to be generous.

After the SD has been formally named in the presence of the very best kind of SDOs, he will start to feel like one of the family, and that involves choosing his 'territory'.

3 *Housing the Sloane Rover*

When the SD comes home, you must expect a few changes around the place. It is no longer *your* home; first and foremost it belongs to the Sloane Dog, for nothing is sacred — furniture, clothes, carpets, toys, food — absolutely nothing.

The present-giving process should start immediately with a basket. This object represents a great deal of wishful thinking on the part of the SDO, for no SD will understand why he has to sleep in a basket while you are sleeping in a bed, but even if it ends up chewed to pieces, the basket is worth a try. Excellent ones are available, ranging in price from several hundred pounds to a paltry few, but the latter do not even bear considering. You would not stint on your own bed, so why stint on your dog's?

As well as the basket itself there are other assorted bits of furniture that need to be dotted about the house to make the SD comfortable. These include a specially-designed, made-to-measure sofa from L. M. Kingcome covered in no-show chintz to co-ordinate with the family furniture (not only does the SD expect his own chair, but this makes sure he keeps off yours), and the Casa Pupo rug at one end of the dining-room for the SD to recline on during those rare occasions when he is not joining the family at dinner (he ate early, doesn't like the menu, etc).

There is also the question of bedding to be considered. Is it to be a duvet, a bean bag, or just a blanket? Which is best, and why? Let the SD decide which he prefers, bearing in mind the following guidelines:

The duvet Tricky. Although an item of great warmth and solace to the average SD this is not recommended for the puppy, or the curious, or the gun dog. This is because the duvet, which should naturally be of the best quality, is filled with feathers — duck feathers. The puppy would rip the cover in a moment of naïve abandon, and try to eat the

28

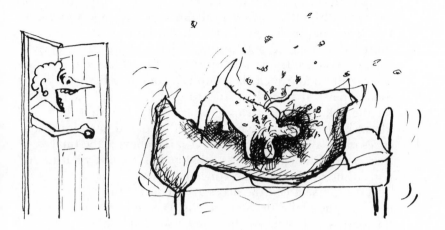

feathers — worrying. The curious SD would simply make a
small hole to investigate the inside of the duvet, and then be
so delighted with the nature of the stuffing it would
undoubtedly rush all over the house exhibiting it. The gun
dog might well suffer a serious psychological trauma trying
to find the ducks, which might result in a blunting of its
natural talents.

The bean bag More an article of furniture than a bedding
item, and extremely popular provided it is well hidden, as it
is often not very attractive. It is a good thing to put in the
ultimate SD kennel (about which more later). Its
disadvantages are similar to those of the duvet except that
the stuffing consists of vast quantities of minute polystyrene
balls — but these at least do not affect the gun dog's sense of
smell.

The blanket The monogrammed blanket has already been
suggested as an excellent christening present, but if your SD
has not received his £600 Atkinson cashmere blanket, you
will be forced to purchase one yourself. There is always the
Sanwald Kamelhair for £250 or — if being forced to skimp
— a Harrods' Ancient Blue Stewart pattern rug for only
£75. The importance of the blanket cannot be too strongly
emphasised; it is the one item that leaves the house regularly
and is seen laid out for the SD to sit on (when he has
forgotten his picnic chair) at events like Ascot, Henley,
Badminton. . . . Need we say more? Folded in the back of the
Range Rover, it proclaims the SD's status for all to see.

Apart from the main furnishings necessary to the arrival of the young SD, there is a very definite 'Starter Kit' to make the young puppy feel at home. This includes a hot-water bottle — cat-shaped ones are available and are particularly useful if you are trying to educate the SD to like cats — and a large Pluto alarm clock (Pluto is a consoling figure to a Sloane pup). It should be stressed that the size of the clock is for the tick, not the alarm — please make sure that the alarm is disengaged or you may well find you have lost your investment after the first night. A large chew is the final item, and although the SD probably won't know what to do with it, he might make an educated guess.

Having assembled the necessary items for the SD's comfort, the major decision now is: Where to put them all for total satisfaction? At this point you could do a breakdown of the possibilities of almost every room in the house, but all you need to do is ask yourself the question: 'Would I sleep in the kitchen/hallway/bathroom/utility room?' No. 'Where is the obvious place to sleep?' The bedroom. Exactly. 'In what?' A bed. Precisely. What more can one add?

Of course, different Sloane homes have different possibilities. A castle in Scotland, for example, may well contain enough rooms for the SD to have his own bedroom, in which case there are no problems — apart from his preference for an antique brass bed. The SD who is sleeping in the grounds of the castle — possibly in multiple accommodation with the rest of the pack — is a different matter. He will have done his military training and be happy to bunk up with the chaps, talking of the old days, remembering the good hunts, the lively parties, drinking his brandy before he goes to sleep and rising with the larks for a good foray before breakfast.

Coming down the scale from the many-roomed castle, there are manor houses and Belgravia mansions, and finally flats, and not many of these will have the space to give the SD his own room, so just as the children, in some cases, may have to share, so does the SD — with you.

Once you have feebly attempted the 'sleeping in another room' approach and the SD has informed you of his inability to sleep anywhere but with you (usually achieved by barking obscenities through whichever door has been shut in his face) — the SD has won.

The next major consideration has to be: Is your bed comfortable enough for the SD? In some cases it will not be and he will resort to his own bed on the other side of the room. If, however, he finds the bed to his taste, then a major education process has to begin to teach him exactly where to lie.

'On' the bed, although it sounds immediately more comfortable, can be deceptive. If the SD is lying ON the bedclothes he greatly restricts movement IN the bed. If there is only one SDO in the bed, the matter is simple — treat the SD as you would any partner. Give it the other side of the bed (in or out, according to preference) and life will be trouble-free. If, however, there are two of you, the problem is quite different. It is an undoubted fact that the most comfortable place in the bed is the point exactly in-between the two groins — and this is certainly the most inconvenient. In this case, immediately purchase a king-size bed (queen-size if room space is prohibitive) and devote the extra space to the SD. If this is not successful, discussions must ensue with the SD to explain the finer points of procreation and the necessity for physical contact between the two SDOs, stressing the need for spontaneity and the inconvenience of having to ask the SD to move every time the moment strikes. (At this point a basic lecture in sex education might well be necessary because SDs are slightly confused about it — see Chapter 13, 'Sex, Drugs and Rock 'n' Roll, page 105 — otherwise it might well go completely over their heads.) The normal outcome of this kind of conversation is that the SD develops a modicum of diplomacy and although he continues to sleep in the between-the-groin position he learns to recognise the signs (the tap of the left shoulder, the touching of the feet — keep it simple) and will happily adjourn to the other side of the room until the disruption is over.

This situation is complicated, however, when the usually single SDO resorts to the occasional 'bit of company'. Not only does the SDO often not take the time to warn the SD of this event, but he may not have explained just what the chaotic behaviour in the night is all about, and this can cause quite serious problems — not the least of which is jealous manslaughter. So a reasonable preparation is essential if you are to avoid a potentially embarrassing scene

between the SD and the new girlfriend/boyfriend/one-night-stand.

    In contrast to the SD who is happy to share its SDO's home, there is the independent SD who craves the responsibility of a mortgage and the management of its own home. But no ordinary home. The SD kennel is a tribute to ultra-modern living, combined with excellent taste. Heated flooring, door locks on the inside (to keep out intruders), electrically-operated security window grilles, insulation throughout, automatic water dispensers with external access, video door entry system to check out guests, intercom connected to the main house to ensure notification of impending mealtimes, and give advance notice of the menu so that he can decide if he wants to partake. When discussing the plans with the SDO the SD stresses that these seemingly extravagant demands are logical and ensure that the SD is protected against weather, war, siege from local cats, dehydration, hypothermia or serious accidents. We have borrowed one design as an example. Note: Speaking from experience one SD has warned us to have a good service contract for all the working items — otherwise the electric window grilles, door entry system and internal door locks can jam, thus making the SD a prisoner in his own kennel. Also make sure the heating is serviced before each winter. (Underfloor heating can be tricky.)

For the interior the SD must be allowed to exercise his own considerable taste — mahogany panelling, leather rather than fabric upholstery (more durable), silk curtains, etc., as well as a good brass door knocker and letter-box, window boxes and two matching bay trees outside the front door (in clay pots brought back by an old JetSD friend, from Spain). These bay trees have a number of uses, including flavouring some of the SD's gourmet cuisine. At this mention of gourmet cuisine we should point out that although great attention to detail will be paid to the interior of the ultimate kennel, a fitted kitchen is not considered necessary as most SDs use the facilities of the SDO's house. A microwave is useful in case the SDOs are out and if the SD desires this item, do not refuse it as it might benefit you in the long run.

Some rural SDs may well prefer the thatched kennel, available from Harrods for £500 upwards, according to size. Custom-built, but along simple country lines — teak veneer, chintz furnishings, no need for central heating — this kennel is for the fresh air SD.

Finally, there is one possibility in the case of a particularly difficult SD which has not been covered. If all the normal offers have been made — the bedroom, the bed, the kennel — and the SD claims that he wants nowhere more than the floor BUT he can't sleep without the SDO, the solution may well be for the SDO to join his SD on the floor. One Sloane owner of three dachshunds, two of which had serious back problems, had to sleep on the floor with them because they could not get on to the bed. His wife, however, continued to sleep at the normal height.

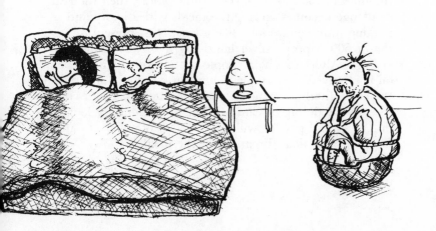

4 *Gourmet Guide*

Food is unquestionably uppermost, nearly all of the time, in the SD's mind. In its most basic form, a bowl of Pedigree Chum or Sainsbury's best is sheer nectar to a peckish pet with simple tastes, and SDs, like SDOs, with simple tastes must be catered for.

THE BASICS

If the SD's tastes do not extend beyond the simple, if he is the nursery-food lover of the canine world, then the real challenge becomes serving the meals with dignity and making humble fare look like a feast. Just presenting it in the £1,500 Asprey's silver hand-engraved bowl might be enough. Alternatively, a simple pottery bowl with his name on is relatively acceptable (when eating alone) and reflects the current ethnic trend in country kitchens. Or, if you feel the solitary dollup of Chum in the ethnic pottery looks too dull, a spot of parsley will add a touch of colour — and improve your dog's breath after the meal.

34

THE LUCKY LAPDOG

A leap up from the basic SD is the steak-or-chicken-breast-and-milk-only SD. He will have an account at the local butchers, with best rump and chicken breast a standard requisite.

Regrettably, however, the occasion may arise where, providing this hardy SD has a healthy appetite, and does not fall into the faddish eater category, a little improvisation may be called for. On those unfortunate evenings when, after a hard day taking Boadicea to the poodle parlour, planning the party list for the birthday party next week, and checking out school prospectuses for the following term's education, you forgot to collect the meat from the butcher — PANIC. this is called the SD-about-to-leave-home-if-I-don't-come-up-with a decent-meal crisis. But fret not — a handy list follows of recipes tried and tested and recommened by the SDOs who know the form. (*Please note, quantities throughout should be related to size of dog and altered accordingly.*)

Daube of Chum (Always keep a tin handy)
A witty little recipe. It won't completely fool the SD, but at least it shows a modicum of effort.

1 tin Pedigree Chum
2 rashers unsmoked bacon
salt & freshly ground pepper
small strip orange peel
(garlic can be added according to the SD's taste)

There is no need to cook the Chum — it's very good as it is (with limitations). In a pan sauté bacon, small amount of garlic (optional) and small chopped strip of orange peel for a few minutes until fat runs and bacon is cooked. Mix this combination in well with the Chum and garnish with grated orange peel.

Delicious and Very Sophisticated Egg Nog (Note the use of the words delicious and sophisticated, which should be repeated continually while preparing this in the face of a bemused SD.)

Dog meal or biscuits
1 egg
½ pint milk
Scotch whisky (optional and only small dash — advantage is it might make dog forget your error)

Place a good layer of dog meal or biscuits on bottom of dish — amount should be judged according to normal feeds.

In a separate bowl beat eggs, milk and whisky (if required) together and pour over the top of the biscuits or meal, mixing slightly to moisten. Keep out of range when you put this down — you may get it thrown at you.

Cornflakes — Delicious and Sophisticated (To be used in desperation)
> Kellogg's Variety Pack (keep in stock with Chum.
> Coco Pops are a particular favourite).

Treat as you would your own breakfast — add sugar if required — and don't just leave the room, leave the house and allow the SD to cool down if he doesn't appreciate your efforts.

Marmite Soldiers (The last resort)
> Bread (brown granary, if possible)
> Marmite
> Butter

Toast bread, apply a lot of butter and Marmite to taste. We stress the need to hand-feed this in order to avoid the SD leaving home.

> The final alternative in the face of SD rejection of the above possibilities is for both you and the SD to go on a fast for a day. It is essential that the SDO does not expect the SD to do it without him.

THE FOODIE PHIDEAUX

> Foodie phideaux are not unlike foodie people and the same foodie code applies to them as to their owners — avoid too-rich sauces, shop regularly at the market, shorten cooking time and consider diet and health. Also, of course, use only the highest quality ingredients. The advantage with the foodie dog is that he can either have a portion of whatever you are having, have a meal of his own as usual, or, if forgotten, will be happy to go without anything at all rather than lower his standards — which makes for a thinner dog, and a much easier crisis situation.
>
> Here are two foodie phideaux suggestions which can be enjoyed by both the SD and the SDO:

Oeufs au Caviare

Take the tops off the eggs very carefully above the roundest part of the shell. Scramble eggs lightly and beat in ½ teaspoon cream, season with salt and pepper and a sprinkling of chopped chives. Spoon mixture back into eggshell and top each one with ½ oz of best caviare. It is suggested that for the SD the penultimate stage be left out — despite the fact that so many SDs love eggshell, some do not — and the mixture transferred straight to the engraved silver bowl.

Rack of Lamb

Prepare as usual, but ensure that for the foodie phideaux the meat is extremely rare — not over twelve minutes to the pound.

THE FADDISH PHIDEAUX

Frankly this is a serious problem, as there is a strong possibility that whatever the fad is it will be extremely awkward. Prawns and kippers only, smoked salmon and baked beans only — Christmas cake and sprats only — that kind of thing.

Naturally, the first advice is TRY NOT TO PANDER TO IT. If you already have, or it was your idea, or he has just picked up on items that you eat anyway, then obviously it is too late. Also, if you are the second owner of a faddish SD then there will be difficulties and your only hope is to purchase a deepfreeze and a microwave to cater for the SD's favourite items. One cannot overstress the importance of this method if the fad is for a seasonal item — total emaciation might otherwise ensue.

THE DIETING DOG

A tragedy — and almost a contradiction in terms. Fat phideaux is an embarrassment to its owner, and a definite problem when it comes to panting round the park. It has to be taken firmly in hand. It is often helpful if the SDO can join the SD on the diet to give him full encouragement. It will probably be difficult for the diets to coincide completely, but we offer on the following page some suggestions as to where they might overlap.

The SD Super Slim Programme — Ten Terrific Tips!

1 No Charbonnel and Walker chocolates, or even Bendicks mints. These are replaced by one Smartie per week.
2 Champagne to be cut down to one glass a week. Perrier instead.
3 Cut down on salt — replace with salt substitutes (the SDO will probably be doing this too which makes it easier).
4 No butter on Marmite soldiers.
5 No more stopping for tea at Richoux.
6 No eating between meals beyond the occasional carrot.
7 No more pasta unless eaten with lemon juice and nothing else (and no more pizzas).
8 Cut down on dining in restaurants — limit to once a day.
9 No cream in the *Oeufs au Caviare*.
10 Attend only one friend's birthday party a week — refuse others politely — more than one kills the effect of the restraint during the rest of the week.

Try and maintain this for at least one month. In addition raise the time spent on the exercise machine (see Chapter 7, 'Exercising Elegantly') and take to walking instead of driving or taking taxis.

The SD might profit from the story of Eos, one of Queen Victoria and Prince Albert's greyhounds which was accidentally shot through the lung by Prince Ferdinand of Saxe-Coburg. Although she recovered she suffered a relapse a year later and the Queen acknowledged that the easy life of over-eating and living in the lap of luxury had weakened her health. 'Now she must be well starved, poor thing,' wrote the Queen, 'and not allowed to sleep in beds as she generally does.' Perish the thought.

THE HEALTHY HOUND

In many cases this will mean being a vegetarian. The SD may have been moved to vegetarianism after seeing SCs (Sloane Cows) go to their fate. Alternatively, he may just dislike meat. There are several alternatives to meat — caviare, for example, is fine, as is fish, though it should preferably be Scotch salmon. The SD may, however, turn up his aristocratic nose at fish, considering it a food for cats and therefore beneath him. Vegetables are no problem and these can be prepared as for the SDO. The Vegetarian Society can always give advice if your SD springs the surprise on you and you don't know how to cope.

To supplement the healthy SD diet there is an excellent range of pills and potions available — items such as Wild Garlic Tablets to increase stamina; Seaweed Mineral Food, supplemented with stinging nettles, rich in iodine and iron for coat, bones and teeth; Charcoal and Aniseed tablets for bad breath; Parsley and Watercress Supplement to aid digestion, and many more.

FUN FOOD FOR SPECIAL OCCASIONS

The Picnic Hamper

Every SDO has to learn how to pack the Ultimate SD Picnic Hamper. It is a must for all those social occasions the SD has to attend, when the fare in the SDO hamper is not to his taste. Out goes the cucumber mousse, tomato salad and potato salad and in comes the *pâté de foie gras*, quails' eggs, Scotch roast beef sliced paper thin and, instead of strawberries and cream, a canine favourite, Charlie's Chocolate Mousse, named after that well-known SD lover King Charles II, and first made as a tribute to him at a King Charles Spaniel Rotary Club Dinner.

The Birthday Party

Every SD expects a good birthday party. All his friends will have very high standards that have developed over the years, and for your SD to fall short of these standards is to bring shame upon the household.

The conscientious SDO will spend some considerable time planning the party. Invitations will have to go out at least a month in advance, otherwise the social SD will be booked up. If your SD is one of the jollier breeds a theme party is not unacceptable — a pink party, blue party, soap opera party, *Lassie Come Home* party, lap-dog party (particularly amusing if most of the guests are Great Danes) — but it is very much up to the individual. What is vital to the party is that none of the essentials listed below is left out.

The birthday cake is the first and most obvious must. There are two approaches to this — one is to make a cake solely for the enjoyment of the SD and his friends, the other is to assume that the SDOs will be eating too and make a cake that they also will enjoy.

Birthday Cake I

     3 lb minced beef steak

     beaten egg, seasoning and breadcrumbs to mix

     For the icing

     1 tube of meat pâté

     1 tube of fish pâté

     large box Ritz crackers

     ½ lb top quality cream cheese

     2 oz Beluga caviare

     1 candle (more is too ostentatious)

The basis of this cake is a high quality pure beef meat loaf.
It is up to individual taste whether this is made round or
square, but it should be of a good, solid consistency and not
too crumbly, so the icing can be added easily. The meat loaf
may be cooked or left raw, according to the SDO's ideas of
how best to feed meat to his dog.

If it is cooked, wait until it is completely cold before
turning it out on to a silver cake-board. Cover it with a
thick layer of the two pâtés in alternating stripes to give a
colourful effect. Stick Ritz crackers in a pattern round the
entire cake. Put the cream cheese in an icing bag and
squeeze a decorative blob into the centre of each cracker,
and into the centre of each blob of cheese place a small
amount of caviare. Place the candle in the top centre Ritz
cracker and cream cheese blob. Pipe a surround of cream
cheese round the base of the cake and for a finishing touch
leave a space on the top of the cake about four Ritz crackers
wide, pipe over it with cream cheese and then write the SD's
name on it in caviare. Do this just before placing the cake
on the table as the black of the caviare tends to run into the
cream cheese.

Birthday Cake II

This is the cake that the SDOs will enjoy too. Start with a
basis of a good chocolate sponge cake (either make this or
buy it from Harrods. Or cheat and buy it from Marks and
Spencers — they make excellent cakes). You can then have
the fun of icing it and decorating to your (and the SD's)
taste.

Theme cakes are quite popular and it is fun to think of
the SD's favourite thing (apart from food), and make the
cake in the shape of it. This may be the Crufts' Best of Show
rosette, or even a silver cup. For the purposes of this

exercise, we give the instructions for the rosette, as it is easier for a first attempt.

Make a standard glacé icing using 8 oz icing sugar to 2 tablespoons of water and use colourings to get the right effect. (Crufts' rosettes are coloured dark and light green.) Coat the cake in dark green icing and then in the lighter green draw a circle approximately 3 inches in diameter in the centre of the cake. Draw lines from this circle to the outside, and emphasise the circle with Smarties. In the centre of the cake in a contrasting colour write 'Happy Birthday' and the SD's name. Cut two pieces of green ribbon $1\frac{1}{2}$ inches wide and 6 inches long and cut a V shape in one end of each. Attach these to the bottom of the cake so they resemble rosette ribbons. Place one candle in the centre of the cake, taking care not to spoil the writing. The cake might well look better than it tastes!

Other party favourites

Sandwiches (no crusts)	Pâté, roast beef, ham, chicken
Jelly	Looks good, cherry is popular or Marmite-flavoured moulded in the shape of a bone.
Blancmange	Pink and cat-shaped — very popular for releasing aggression.
Truffles	Covered in chocolate vermicelli.
Flapjacks	Good for regularity.

Peripheral delicacies

Smarties	Crisps	Liquorice allsorts
Potato hoops	Cheese balls	Cocktail sausages

To finish off the party in style it is absolutely essential that every SD has a 'goody bag' to take home that both they and their SDO can share. Many parties are judged on the merit of their 'goody bags' and they should include some or all of the following:

Balloons for blowing up at home and keeping in the mood.
Quarter bottle of champagne.
Any spare pieces of cake (only if it's bearable).
A champagne swizzle stick.
1 oz of caviare, a box of Smarties... and so on, varying according to status of, and number of guests.

DRINKS

This poses quite a dilemma — do we serve champagne as well as water and/or milk — particularly for the celebratory toast? Frankly, this is totally up to the individual SD — some may find champagne bubbles daunting and prefer a glass of port after the meal instead. (Note: If serving champagne, the wide 'saucer'-type glasses are the perfect shape and height to serve it in and are much favoured by the average SD.)

Perhaps a cocktail is preferred? The Roof Gardens Restaurant in Kensington has devised one specially for the SD called **Rover's Revenge:**

> Glass of champagne
> Dash of blue curaçao
> Serve with decorative slice of orange.

Or **Hair of the Dog:**

> 1 oz Scotch
> 1¼ oz heavy cream
> ½ oz honey
> Shake vigorously with shaved ice and strain into cocktail glass.

The **Bullshot** is a popular SD cocktail:

> 1 can Campbell's condensed consommé
> 2 oz vodka
> Teaspoon Worcester sauce, juice of half a lemon.
> Mix vigorously with plenty of ice and strain into big glass.

EVERYDAY TREATS

Part and parcel of a Sloane Dog's daily gourmet experiences are his 'treats', for without them the SD knows he has no reason to do anything anyone requires of him.

There are two categories of treats, sweet and savoury, and every SD has his favourite. In the sweet range chocolates are definitely a major weakness (the Sloane Dog prefers those from Fortnums, Bendicks and Charbonnel and Walker). Savoury treats are such goodies as a nice piece of roast sirloin or fillet steak, a sliver of roast pheasant, a piece of Roquefort, and so on. Most items on the party food list fall into the category of treats and these may be cheaper alternatives for the hard-pressed SDO — crisps, peanuts (dry roasted), potato hoops, etc.

Finally, there is the bone. To get the best bone the SD or his owner must learn to cultivate a local butcher, and if he can't be cultivated then he should no longer be patronised.

EATING OUT

Most Sloane Dogs are very happy eating out in restaurants favoured by their owners — the only problem being that not all restaurateurs are as enthusiastic. From jet-setting SDs we have reports of two particularly good SD-only restaurants: In Chicago, Famous Fido's Doggie Deli sells gourmet fare such as Chicken à la Fido and Kidney Ragout, followed by dessert cookies. None of the cookies includes sugar or preservatives. The Deli hosts birthday parties and organises Fido Grams and Pup Party Take-out Kits. Secondly, in Nice, the Beach Regency Hotel has a separate dining-room for SDs with an excellent menu including special biscuits, pastries and a superb selection of cocktails. They also speak English, which is most convenient.

5 *Canine Couture*

The fashionably attired Sloane Dog is not a recent phenomenon. Throughout history SDs — particularly the smaller breeds — have been valued as playthings and companions of royalty, aristocracy and society. Along the trade routes of the ancient world myriads of SDs accompanied by sumptuous accessories were presented as gifts to emperors and kings. Burial chambers dating from the days of the Pharaohs have revealed the vestiges of diminutive dogs wearing ornate collars. In ancient Rome they wore collars of gold and coral. In cold weather they were covered with golden cloth and carried by slaves for their 'walks' with their owners. In addition SDs acted as *postillons d'amour*, carrying messages in their collars to their mistresses' secret lovers.

From the seventeeth century on, London and Paris became the centres for canine couture. Jewellers produced costly trifles to please owners. Parisian poodles wore bracelets of gold and silver studded with jewels; raincoats and furs were designed to protect dogs from cold and rheumatism. Fashion magazines were available at the exclusive canine couturiers where society dogs were offered titbits on silver plates while their owners contemplated the latest styles.

Alas, times have changed. The SD fantasy of a luxurious and bejewelled life is but a dream, and canine couture now falls into two categories — the kind of clothes worn by the traditional SD, with its greatest extravagance being a pearl collar, and its norm a disintegrating leather strap; and those worn by what is considered to be the eccentric SD, which is none the less Sloane in nature, but has taken a wilder path.

Shrugging aside the barrage of contradictory views on the subject with only one comment — if your SD lives, as you do, in a centrally-heated home, sleeps, as you do, in an antique brass bed under a duvet, why shouldn't he get cold as you do when he goes out? — we launch straight into the subject of clothes. We begin with a hour by hour guide to what the best-dressed eccentric SD (ESD) is wearing.

No such SD would be seen at breakfast without his monogrammed robe and a copy of the *Financial Times**.

*The SD often develops an interest in newspapers when he is being trained in his earliest days.

Although the traditional Noel Coward style of silk dressing-gown is much favoured, we recommend that the current fashion for towelling robes — in tasteful dark blue with gold piping — should be taken full advantage of. However well-mannered the SD is, the cleaning bills with silk can become quite out of hand.

Following breakfast, and a rigorous brush with his monogrammed tortoisehell brush and comb set, the SD prepares to take the first exercise of the day. For this, the jogging suit is ideal. Harrods do one with its own hood for chilly mornings, or alternatively for an indoor workout, just fluorescent legwarmers and a short-sleeved matching tee shirt.

Naturally by this point the country SD would probably have taken a different route — simply slipping on his Husky or Barbour and possibly his green wellingtons, and plunging forth into hearty countryside for a good brisk walk, stopping off at the pub for lunch on the way home.

Meanwhile back in London, the SD returns to the bedroom after the workout, or the gentle jog round the park, to prepare for lunch. Lunch on the whole is a casual affair, often meeting up with SDs who are working — perhaps in-between modelling assignments or off-duty from guarding the nearby department store (e.g. Harrods, or Harvey Nichols or Peter Jones), and clothes really should match the occasion, and be easy to take on and off if a shopping spree is to follow lunch. We recommend staying with the casual sweatshirt look — with or without designer label — but in a good strong colour which could even match that of the SDO. For a more formal lunch the navy sweatshirt with the familiar gold piping and a Hermes scarf is eminently suitable. Unfortunately the occasion will arise when the SDO cannot take the SD to lunch with him or her — it has to be accepted that some restaurants just won't let the SD in, and when this happens we recommend the SD has a shower after its exercise, puts on a casual tracksuit, has a glass of champagne and uses the time to catch up with some petit point, paint paw nails, or check the stock market.

After lunch is the time for shopping and picking up the juiest gossip at the best parks (see pp. 60–62 on where to go). There is often not much chance to change clothes, but if going out straight from home and going to a park as well —

in the summer aim for something light (the current trend for vests is useful), but for a winter stroll choose something warm. The choice is enormous, from leopard coat through Daks raincoat to tartan-lined sheepskin. Or even a Sherlock Holmes-style cape and hat would be fitting — again available from Harrods.

On the way home from the afternoon's spree SDs pop in and choose their favourite pastries from Richoux to take home for tea, which they enjoy with cucumber sandwiches and Earl Grey from Fortnum and Mason.

Tea over, it's back to the bedroom to prepare for the evening. It is now that the importance of the SD's sleeping quarters becomes so apparent — it must feel it has a place to go in the daytime, when perhaps the rest of the house is in chaos.

For the evening, subtlety is of the essence, and it is at this point that the male and female SDs part ways. Up until now the clothes have been similar for both, but now the male reaches for his bow tie and wing collar and the female for her strand of pearls, or for the very lucky lady, a single strand of diamonds. Fortunately the fashion for costume jewellery makes the situation easier (and cheaper) and some of the currently popular diamanté necklaces are very fetching. These items can be worn for everything from the dinner at home to the serious cocktail party, and indeed are still suitable if going on to a club later in the evening.

The evening slides wickedly into parties, and heavy nights on the town. Scope here is enormous and depends very much on the nature of the SD — the young male will probably just stick to his bow tie, or if the evening is truly eccentric he might don his pulsating flashing collar which only lights up when he moves and causes much hilarity amongst his friends. His female friend can wear one of these too, but is more likely to prefer the pearls or diamanté (branching out into Butler and Wilson for more glitz), or to go to town in taffeta, net, silk and beading, and really make an impression. The main disadvantage with the outrageous outfit is that it can be worn only once, for everyone will recognize it the second time. As with all good taste, simplicity is best.

And so the day is over, the night played out, and the weary SD prepares to hit the sack. Teeth are cleaned, one hundred strokes are brushed through long hair, prayers are said, make-up removed, and naked as the day it was born, the SD falls asleep. Pyjamas and nightdresses are quite acceptable, but surveys show that most dogs prefer to sleep *au naturel*.

On the continent, of course, the SD's day varies, owing to the tendency for Europeans to take an afternoon nap and achieve their shopping in the evening. This delights the continental SD who loves to snooze, and who is only too happy to alternate its shopping bouts with periods sitting in cafés and watching the world go by. In America, too, the behaviour is different — in many cases the shops stay open later, everything is bigger, and no self-respecting SD would be seen without a designer-label on everything.

There is one problem which arises frequently and which should be tackled in this chapter — and that is, how to cope when the SD is refused entry to an establishment. One solution, which is not foolproof, but can often be a great help, is to carry the SD into the establishment in a basket. A shoulder basket is highly suitable, but please note this only applies to a small SD, and we are not advocating risking a dislocated shoulder by trying to carry a Labrador into a restaurant in this way. Good baskets are not at all easy to find and naturally the comfort of the SD (who may well find this a great slur on his dignity as it is) is the first priority, so the basket or bag should have a good base. Scout all the obvious places first — Harrods, Peter Jones, Heals, Liberty's and finally Louis Vuitton, who has been known to make them, and who showed one in a recent exhibition in the Dog Museum of New York called 'Pampered Pets'. If all else fails, you may have to have one made, and some design points are illustrated.

One SD who lived in a hotel that did not allow dogs, whether Sloane or not, spent large periods of his life in a shoulder basket, being carried in and out. Apart from the occasional *faux pas* in the lift when he wanted to ask a question and therefore popped his head out, he got quite used to snoozing on the move, and found it very comfortable. Indeed, he was later heard to say he found walking rather tiring.

Two more useful accessories in the SD's day-to-day life are the car seat — which is designed to keep the SD high

enough to see easily out of the windows, and offers excellent security when the SDO takes a sudden left; and, for sailing SDs, the life-jacket, which is a valuable addition to the essentials that should be on board all SD-carrying vessels. With adjustable buckles for a snug fit and a great design improvement on models of old, this can be worn all the time the SD is on the boat, and greatly reduces the risk of drowning when he has fallen off the boat.

The traditional SD, on the other hand, may well not be so interested in the trivia of dressing up. This SD enjoys the outdoor life, enjoys a chance to get really dirty and have a jolly good time. He will undoubtedly have, at the very least, a traditional plaited collar and lead, or, at the very most, a Gucci collar and lead. Whether the SD needs a lead at all is a matter of some dispute. In the country it is not even considered, but in London it is necessary when ignorant passers-by separate the SD and the SDO in a busy street and traffic becomes a major hazard. Collars and leads are a difficult area to define from the SD point of view. What is correct and what isn't? Usually it can be taken for granted that most people buy a collar and lead out of necessity and hope they will not have to buy one again for a long time. On this basis the best leather, the best buckles and the strongest lead are undoubtedly what are wanted. For fashion purposes it is good if the SD's collar and lead match the SDO's outfits — indeed, if the SD wears many clothes they should all co-ordinate with the SDO's outfits.

The best collars and leads are, of course, made to measure in the finest Italian leather and monogrammed.

Dog tags are another item that may have been given as a christening present, and a good silver or gold identity disc in a simple typeface with the SDO's name and address on it is always an appealing idea. SDs have never been able to understand why SDOs don't have identity discs or papers also — it seems such an obvious idea and one that is standard in many other countries in the world.

Naturally there are items of great value to both the ESD and the TSD (traditional Sloane dog). These include the wellington boot — in many cases this looks more like a wellington sock with a woollen upper piece for warmth and to keep it on more tightly, but there are some excellent red wellingtons available from America which cause great hilarity with chums in Hyde Park.

Then there is a wonderful invention called the Dri Dog Bag. It is literally a large bag lined with towelling that the lucky, filthy wet SD leaps into as he reaches the car or house or wherever it is he is not supposed to make dirty. The ESD likes it because he can take off his wet clothes and creep modestly into the bag, which keeps him warm and dries him off until he has time to dash into the shower and freshen up. The TSD like it because it means he can get very dirty indeed and extremely wet and no one will complain because he's tucked in the bag and cannot make a mess.

Inevitably there is the ultimate SD who will totally co-ordinate, not just with the SDO's outfit, but with his car as well. If the car is not a Rover, which is after all quite understandable, then the SD will ensure that a bronze effigy of itself is mounted on the bonnet so that everyone is aware of its importance when they are stuck in traffic jams, or at the lights. This is considered quite acceptable ostentation.

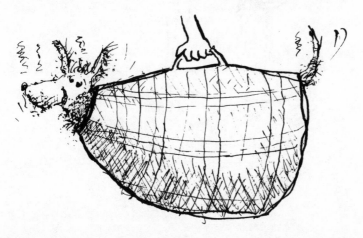

6 Correct Coiffure

Couture and coiffure go hand in hand (or paw in paw).
After talking with several SDs it transpires that coiffure for
the average SD on the street varies considerably from that of
the Show SD. The Show SD has his own chapter later in the
book, but it is the products that have been developed for
him that the SD on the street now takes full advantage of.
The serious SD requests early on in life that his SDO take
him to Peter's Posh Pets in Blythe Road, West Kensington
(or to his own particular favourite spot, nearer home) where
he can not only wallow in self-indulgence, but meet other
SDs (or in some cases not so Sloane dogs) from every walk of
life — and the SD does love a chance to increase his social
circle. This also means that SD and SDO can put their faith
in someone else's expertise and have it all done for them.

The following products come to us with glowing recommendations from far and wide among our SD acquaintances. Doreen Page's Natural Skincare Products include the magnificent Oil of Peach shampoo, with extra rich lather and delicate perfume, or there is the Captured style spray for coping with that fly-away coat. Rapport, too, make a terrific coat spray — the choice is purely personal (also their Sour Grapes Liquid Chewing Repellent is a great help to the SDO trying to control a nibbling SD). The Beapher Natural range is a pure health range and includes the highly recommended Mink Oil for Long Hair shampoo, and Gold with Iodine shampoo, for a gleaming coat. (Beapher also do an excellent range of health tablets for the inner dog.) If the SD runs out of its own products it can use those of its long-suffering owner, but most SDs prefer not to do so, as their skins are so delicate and they worry about the products causing them irritation.

When it comes to colour, the SDs, like the SDOs, naturally have what they were born with, ranging from white through tricolour and red to black. Occasionally, when the young SD is going through a rebellious phase, or for modelling assignments, it might be necessary to add a livelier colour to the hair to complete the SD's image or to complement an item in a photograph. In order to make the SD feel more at ease when its SDO approaches it with a paint brush, we have taken advice as to the best products to use and how to use them.

Firstly, crazy colours may be harder to remove than some others, and a product developed specifically for the SD craving colour in his life is the range of Pets' Paradise hair dyes with evocative names such as Pungent Purple, Brilliant Blue and Lime Green, and these are easy to apply and completely non-toxic. They wash in just like shampoo, and providing care is taken with application should provide an even and vivid hue when finished. (Just a weeny word of warning: these colours might not wash out completely on the first wash — or indeed even on the second, and one or two SDs have had to endure rude jests from park-walking peers when the modelling assignment is over and they are still a strong shade of Paradise Pink!)

Some young SDOs may want to have their SD's hair cut in the same style as their own. Well, again, this is not

impossible, providing the hairdresser is amenable. There is no harm in giving a King Charles a Mohican haircut, but it might be worth asking his opinion about it first as it might, frankly, just not suit him at all. For plenty of scope the best breed to choose is the Chinese Crested which has a Mohican to start with.

Canine coiffure is well catered for, and there is a wealth of equipment to choose from for the ultimate look. If the SD was not lucky enough to receive a tortoiseshell dressing-table set for its christening present, there is no need to despair; there is a good selection of alternatives ranging from the ultimate Universal Dog Brush to less well-known comb-and-brush-in-one sets, to matching monogrammed sets. In addition, of course, there are curling tongs (cordless are preferable when trying to crimp the SD who will be answering the telephone and rushing around the house at the same time), and a large variety of special hairdriers.

Of all SDs the poodle has long been the most coiffure-conscious, and this sound little breed is used to spending many a day in the poodle parlour. An SD just starting on the road to beauty could do worse than invite a poodle to lunch to discuss the pros and cons and heed its advice — there's not much it will not know about grooming.

Apart from the high quality brush and comb, the hairdrier and the curling tongs, the SD's beauty basics should include:
— A good selection of nail varnishes, for perfect colour co-ordination.
— Toothpaste, toothbrush and toothpicks for perfect pearlies.
— Amplex tablets or Gold Spot for glorious breath.
— A good manicure set.
— A good mirror surrounded by lights — very Hollywood, but a definite aid to put the SD in the mood for beauty.
— Tenax *fixateur pour cheveux* (hair fixative) is a must for the 1920s slicked-down look.

The current fashion trend seems to be for the natural look — shaggy and wild. Hair extensions are always a possibility, although many dogs — the Puli, for example — don't need any artificial aids. Luckily this natural look caters well for the county SD who has always subscribed to it anyway.

Although the Show SD has its own chapter, a section on coiffure would not be complete without mentioning the time and effort that goes into perfecting the show dog for its competitions. This is not just a one-day session at Peter's

Posh Pets — it is a daily routine requiring diligence and great discipline. No SD should think he can make it without applying himself first — it is not a matter of just popping in and winning. We recommend that any SD considering this path has a serious chat with a current professional — besides, there are secrets to be learnt which we could not get anyone to reveal to us!

Finally, we must not forget that outer beauty depends upon inner well-being. For this we look to Ginseng for libido, Royal Jelly for eternal youth, Vitamin E for glowing skin, Oil of Evening Primrose to counter the effects of female tension (amongst other things), and calcium compounds for healthy teeth and bones.

If, however, nothing seems to work, and the coat is still lank and dull, you will have to resort to an age-old remedy used by SDs and SDOs alike (and one of the few tips we managed to extract from an old-timer show champion): take a silk scarf and rub the coat with it several times — it should positively gleam!

7 *Exercising Elegantly*

Exercise, along with food, is an SD essential. Enthusiasm does not run as high for exercise as for food, but nonetheless it is a major factor in the health and happiness of the SD.

Exercise can be taken in many different ways according to the nature of both the dog and the owner.

The Slow Stroll

This manner of exercise is usually taken by the elderly, infirm, convalescing or posing SD. It is not ideal, but is definitely better than nothing. (It is also taken by the lazy SD, but that does not bear mentioning.) Slow strolling is better in scenic areas, and is frequently well suited to parks where dogs must remain on leads such as parts of Holland Park and Regent's Park, or indeed to the Nice Promenade. It is, of course, also ideal for the short-legged SD, SDOs (or even SDs) in high heels, and for those SDs doing *la passeggiata*.

The Jolly Jog

Jolly jogger SDs and SDOs like to get a burst of exercise over with early in the day, then relax without conscience.

The jolly jogger SDO is in some ways being lazy by taking the SD with him, as it saves him an extra excursion with the dog, but providing the SD is a jolly jogger too there is absolutely no problem. The JJSD usually wears his leg warmers to coordinate with those of the JJSDO so that if they get separated someone will probably be able to direct them to each other. Separation is very likely as both SD and SDO tend to wear their Sony Walkman's, but with different music on and they inevitably fall out of step.

The Chuck and Chase Brigade

This is the ideal solution for the zappy SD who is accompanied by a slothful SDO. It gives the SDO a relaxed stroll, and the SD an excellent run for his money. The missile is not usually important, but inevitably varies with the size of the dog — a small SD will go wild for a golf ball or a conker (when in season) but beware throwing the larger SD either of these, as the only way it will return to sender is in the dog's tummy. Sticks are the traditional thing to throw, but do have the disadvantage of being eminently chewable. If hurling in parks, do it on the path, since it not only exercises the SD but wears down its nails at the same time. Naturally, if given the choice, the SD would probably rather chase a Bendicks mint — but, of course, that would never be brought back. (A warning to the chuckers — don't chuck anywhere near any other SDOs or you may find yourself in court.)

Towing

This is not recommended, but we mention it since many people do it and it cannot therefore be overlooked. The SDO doesn't get out of his car and the SD is trailed on a long extending lead out of the back of the car. This is not kind. Quite acceptable, on the other hand, is the SDO on a bicycle and the SD just following behind. Susannah York and her King Charles, Archie, used to exercise this way. Another acceptable version is the SDO on a horse and the SD following on behind, which is a very common sight in Richmond Park. The whole practice is not unsatisfactory provided the SD is not actually attached to the vehicle or horse. It is, however, only really recommended if the SDO is extremely ill or cannot walk at all and no alternatives are available.

Swimming

Swimming is, of course, a delight and a pleasure to the SD and the SDO, particularly if it can be undertaken in water above 67 degrees. It is not easy for the SD to enjoy a good swim in any of the London swimming pools, as the RAC don't let in women let alone SDs (male or female) and the Lansdowne is not too keen either. So there are really only two possibilities — public ponds such as the Round Pond, Serpentine and such like (but, of course, the SDO is not likely to join in), or the private pool. The heated indoor pool in one's own grounds is ideal.

Indoor Exercise

The fitness craze has hit not just the average SDO, but also the SD, with full force. One of life's pleasures for the SD is to be able to accompany the SDO on most of his journeys through life, and the gymnasium is no exception, but utilizing the equipment to the full in the gym has to be done with care or serious injury to the SD can ensue. The equipment that the SD has no trouble with are the parallel bars (excellent for balance); rope climbing (strengthens the teeth and paws admirably, although Sloane cats tend to prefer this); the mini trampoline (very popular at the moment); and the wall bars (marvellous for back exercises). However, the ultimate piece of equipment is the jogging machine, and this is certainly a must for every SD home as it can be a godsend when it's too wet to go out or when you are snowed in. Aerobics classes provide an excellent release for the SD at the end of a heavy day, and providing some favourite music is used ('Hound Dog', 'Walking the Dog', anything from *Cats* to rouse the adrenalin), the SD will shake and shimmy with the best of them.

If the SD is lucky enough to live in Los Angeles he might be a member of Beverly's Doggerie and Animal Center which is a health spa for pets boasting a sauna, jacuzzi and all the other essential exercise aids. Beverly, the proprietor, says that you can't walk dogs in LA because of the riff-raff on the streets, and the beach is no good because the little USASDs all drown, so what alternative is there? The best part about it is that you can rub paws with the pooches of the stars...

Squash and Tennis

These two sports elude the SD due to the complications which arise over holding a racquet.

WHICH PARK?

The park is, of course, the perfect spot for the best exercise. What is a park without its elegantly exercising SDs? But no SD will go to just any park — the burning question is, *which park?* Given a choice, all SDs would name a royal park — they have, after all, been walking in royal parks for many years with many royal personages, but, alas, it is not always possible to choose one's park so selectively; inevitably proximity has a certain amount to do with it. However, we give a brief park guide below and list a few acceptable alternatives to the royal park throughout the world.

St James's Park Unquestionably the most royal royal park, located as it is in the centre of a veritable plethora of palaces. King Charles II had a major influence on its appearance, which he based on parks he had seen on his travels. One of his dogs was stolen in Pall Mall (named after the game Paile Maile): 'Lost four or five days since in St James's Park, dogg of his Majestie's, full of blew spots with a white cross on his forehead and about the bigness of a tumbler. . . . ' Naturally St James's is the SD King Charles Spaniel's favourite haunt.

Green Park In 1938, a balloonist named Mrs Graham made an ascent from Green Park as part of the Coronation festivities. This ended in a fatal accident when the balloon's grapnel tore one of the coping stones off the roof of a house in Marylebone, causing the death of a passer-by. Happily no SDs were injured.

Hyde Park An historically popular spot for duelling — Labradors seen with pistols at dawn? Tyburn gallows nearby — SDs don't hang around. An attempt was made on King George III's life in this park but it was unsuccessful and yet again, no SDs were involved.

Hyde Park

Kensington Gardens The poetic park: 'Love, spring and Kensington Gardens, hey for the heart's delight'. Peter Pan is resident here but not Nana who, providing she was Norland, really was an SD.

Regent's Park Once part of the Forest of Middlesex. The Zoo makes it a particularly attractive diversion for the SD. In 1867 crowds skating on the lake fell in and drowned, and eight years later a chain of barges carrying gunpowder blew up and damaged the Macclesfield Bridge and canals. SDs be warned — don't skate or carry gunpowder.

Richmond Park An out-of-the-centre SD haunt. Used to be a major source of royal venison — gives SDs food for thought while strolling round.

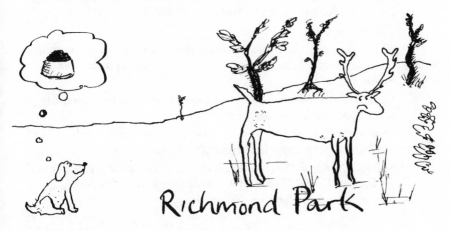

Richmond Park

Greenwich Park Further out still, but very historical — there has been human settlement (and no doubt, therefore, canine settlement) for 2,000 years on this spot.

SOME NON-ROYAL, BUT ACCEPTABLE SPOTS

Hampstead Heath — Michael Foot walks Dizzy here!

Putney Common — follow in the footsteps of SD favourite, Jilly Cooper's dogs.

Wimbledon Common — walk with the Wombles.

Barnes Common — a lot of Sloane actors walk their dogs here.

Clapham Common — may not sound Sloane but you'd be surprised who lives near it.

Battersea Park — Capability Brown liked it, so why not?

Wandsworth Common — again, an un-Sloane name but getting Sloaner by the minute.

Bois de Boulogne, Paris — only experienced by JetSDs and the French, but a blissful place.

Central Park, New York — the ultimate USASD walking spot. The park — if it's not happening in Central Park, it's not happening.

Nice Promenade — not a park but a superlative spot for *la passeggiata*. Get out the gold lamé and slingbacks for this little stroll.

The Square, Monte Carlo — dress down rather than up.

Hyde Park, Sydney — small compared with ours but a park is a park (beaches better in Australia). This park was first used for military drill, cricket and horse racing.

The Borghese Gardens, Rome — steeped in history.

Ardene Gardens, Cape Town — should you be passing, a small park in eighteenth-century style with a unique collection of exotic trees.

Olympic Park, Montreal — for a good run with the spirit of the Olympics in the air.

Stanley Park, Vancouver — some say the best park in the world — sea on three sides and mountains on the other.

Sydney's National Parks — if Hyde Park in Sydney is too small go for the Royal National Park in the south of Ku-ring-gai Chase National Park in the north.

8 *Elementary Education*

The education of the SD has been covered fully by many wise pet educators, including the SDOs all-time favourite, Barbara Woodhouse, so in this chapter we are taking a broader and more general approach to the subject and considering some of the social graces that may sometimes be overlooked.

As the SD has undoubtedly already taken over your home, it is quite essential that he behaves correctly and adopts some fundamental manners, in the interests of maintaining domestic harmony. In a perfect world the ideal SD would be able to hunt down thieves, collect the Sunday papers, get the children ready for school, do the ironing and take itself for a walk. Alas, such expectations are seldom, if ever, realised.

It is a real bonus if the basic communication channels can be opened with such simple commands as 'No!' 'Sit!' 'Stay!' and 'Good!' However, the average SD tends to treat such basic instructions with contempt and will undoubtedly ignore them, though it is still worth a try. More important than these simple commands is the instilling of elementary good manners.

63

Good manners begin with no begging. The SD circling
the dining-table like a lone shark round a drowning sailor,
gazing hopefully at everyone, and finally leaping on to the
lap of the likeliest-looking candidate out of sheer
desperation, is to be discouraged — particularly as he has
probably just been enjoying an excellent meal at Langan's
or *nouvelle cuisine* in the nursery with his chums. (Some
SDs may merely hint, and this is quite acceptable.)

Another habit that has to be nipped in the bud — and
one that is particularly prevalent in large dogs, as they are
built for the crime — is stealing. The plump, trussed turkey
at Christmas; the six chocolate mousses — worse, the Boeuf
Stroganoff — polished off just as you are finishing the first
course of your dinner party; the crisps, peanuts and sundry
items left on the coffee table and snaffled by SDs of a lesser
build; such crimes are not to be tolerated. The latter variety
of theft is greatly aided by the SDO ratlet who acts as an
accessory to the crime either by passing the goodies over to
the SD on the spot, or by taking them out of the room so
that the SD can get hold of them out of sight and earshot of
the grown-ups.

After begging and stealing, dirt and the random gathering
of it is the next major problem. It is as well to try to explain
that dirt is absolutely not wanted in any of the rooms of the
house and must remain in or on the garden, or on the
welcome mat. Teach him to wipe his paws every time he
comes in. The SD with his own luxury kennel will probably
appreciate this immediately as he will have to do his
housework (unless you have provided him with his own

cleaner, and we do think this is excessive), but the SD who is
waited on hand and foot (or paw and tail) may need firmer
guidance.

Other manners which need to be instilled are: refraining
from picking his nose, brushing his teeth morning and night,
learning to stand at a cocktail party with a plate of food in
one hand and a glass in the other without throwing them
over everyone, and various other social niceties that must
become second nature. Once these are imprinted on the
SD has begun to acquire some of the *savoir faire* that you
further education.

As there is not currently a school fees plan for the SD,
many SDOs will choose to educate the SD at home rather
than sending him away to school. This also avoids the
uniform costs and the buying of a large trunk and tuck box
for school terms. So for those noble SDOs about to tackle
the problem of education at home, we offer a few helpful
hints.

Chocolate (Bendicks, Charbonnel and Walker, etc.) is a
great leveller. In the early stages, as an economy, chocolate
buttons (and choc drops) are quite acceptable, but once the
SD has begun to acquire some of the *savoir faire* that you
are trying to impart to him, then nothing but the best will
do. The SD is much more amenable to doing things he
would otherwise not consider, when bribed with a good
bittermint.

Tranquillizers are the next essential — predominantly for
you for when he eats or digs up the neighbours' plants,

terrorises the neighbourhood cats, molests a very smart local bitch, deposits unfortunate evidence of his presence in Jaeger (for some reason many children seem to choose Jaeger — probably the SD will too), runs riot at the village fête, or knocks over ten antique champagne glasses with his tail at your best friend's engagement party. Another early phase which can induce the vapours in the SDO is randiness in the male — and for more details of this see Chapter 13, 'Sex, Drugs and Rock 'n' Roll', page 105.

We suggest that you enrol yourself in yoga classes to relieve the strain and acquire techniques for relaxation and inner calm. Then impart to the SD some of the yoga you have just learned so that he too learns to remain calm. The lotus position is excellent for sharpening the concentration.

Remember — violence is not the answer. Do not take classes in judo or karate whilst in the early stages of educating your SD because there is a very high probability that you will hurl him across the room or chop him in half with your bare hands at the least sign of insubordination.

If all attempts at educating your SD fail, do not be ashamed if you find out you have a psychotic dog on your hands. Roger Mugford, the well-known dog psychiatrist, will give advice as to how best to cope with some of the problems the SD might have. The Yellow Pages have lists of people who will be happy to help in the case of the SDO being overburdened with problems.

If, right at the beginning of the education process, you feel you are not going to be able to devote adequate time to it, or if you feel you are unable to bring out the best in your SD, then a nanny is the best solution. A well-trained nanny will instil the essential disciplinary points with ease — such as keeping elbows off the rim of the bowl, basic dancing steps, how to behave in public places, and so on.

If you decide to send the SD to school, there are many to choose from. As any SD will tell you, however, it is not just a matter of educating him, but of forming his character. A good school instils discipline and determination in its pupils. Cold showers, learning not to trust the opposite sex, learning not to sneak on the chum who couldn't wait to get to the kerb, and meeting dogs who will be useful in later life, will result in a finely-tuned canine machine.

Some SDs who have received their education at home

COUNTRY LIFE

Bride of the month

choose to go to a 'finishing school' abroad to learn to ski, pick up a new language and some useful chums, and then use the six months in quarantine to perfect these newly acquired graces.

It is delightful for both the SD and the SDO to be able to show off their mutual achievement at the end of the training period, either at a small 'Coming Out' drinks party to which some close friends and their SDs are invited, or at a real Coming Out party, where it might be amusing to show off the young SD's social skills and behaviour.

For the Coming Out party, whichever way the SDO chooses to go about it, the SD is able to wear his first bow-tie, or her first pearls. The manners that will really show the past few months' work are the ability to circulate quietly as people arrive without tripping them up or attracting unnecessary attention; not letting a wagging tail knock any glasses off any tables; not opening its mouth the entire evening except perhaps for a gentle yawn behind a paw; not drinking too much champagne (as this is the first time the SD has been let loose with unlimited champagne, apart from the one glass at the christening, the SDO may have to keep an eye on him — leglessness on the big night out would be most unsavoury); and finally, sitting quietly throughout dinner and only biting someone's ankle as a gentle reminder if that person tries to pass the port the wrong way at the end of the meal.

The Coming Out party over, the SD will naturally go for a sitting to have its photograph taken by a well-known society photographer, who will take some very tasteful shots for the top of the piano, the Gucci wallet, and for the odd social column — perhaps even *Country Life*.

Once launched, the complete social diary is open to the SD who can whirl and shimmy his way through event after event, from horse trials to polo, from Crufts to Ascot, from Henley to balls and clubs and back to horse trials.

Of course, once the invitations start pouring in, one of the essentials is to be able to write a good letter of acceptance or refusal. One feature of the SD's letter is that it does require the assistance of the SDO to provide the graphic talent, with the SD adding a pawprint signature at the bottom. As an example we include a letter written by an excellent SD of outstanding character, which shows a superb style and

MARY QUANT
Limited

Gigot Plunket Greene thanks
Francesca Findlater for her
kind invitation for May 11th
but regrets he must refuse
as he is lunching at the
Tomb* with his godfather,
Bustopher Jones.

*

on cabbage, rice-pudding and mutton.

Directors: Mary Quant, O.B.E., R.D.I., F.S.I.A., Archie McNair (Chairman), Ian Lyle, M.B.A. (Managing), Alexander Plunket Greene, Catherine McNair, Peter Dunkerley, John Rowlerson
Registered Office: Address as Above Registered in England. Registration No. 784001

charming originality. We are not suggesting this letter be copied slavishly, rather that it should be used as an illustration of the value of developing a personal style.

As well as knowing how to behave at parties and how to write a good letter there are other little things the SD should be seen to do to ensure his lifestyle remains suitably Sloane.

- When your SDO next organises a charity 'do', offer your services to run a stall. For example 'Stop the Ball' has been suggested by one SD. The rules are as follows: the Sloane participant buys three balls for... (amount left to organiser's discretion); he has to throw the balls into a bucket BUT the SD has to catch them and prevent them from going in the bucket. Only three in the bucket wins.
- If your SDO is not totally on the right lines, then it is often your duty as a good SD to help her. If her garden, for example, is dotted with crazy paving (horror), dig it up. If there is no croquet lawn, cultivate one. (The SD in a flat is restricted, but nonetheless even the window boxes should look Sloanely spontaneous.)
- If you feel your SDO does not dress correctly, or is wearing and unSloane shade of lipstick, then you as an SD are in an excellent position to deal with the situation: eat the offending article. If a crimplene object enters the house — destroy!
- It is your duty as an SD to project and perpetuate the Sloane image.

Once the SD is educated, the world is his oyster. Some SDs can wallow in the lap of luxury for the rest of their lives, but for others the future is harder — they have to find a job.

9 Gainful Employment

There are several reasons why the SD might take up employment. Some, who want to feel they are keeping up with the times, get a job so they can afford the odd bauble, and have something to talk about at Kennel Club dinners. Some enjoy being useful and meeting people, and involve themselves in voluntary work. Some SDs, however, have to face facts — they have to go out to work to earn their living. C.M. McMuck, the King Charles author of *Top Dog*, is not in favour of the SD going to work — but sadly often needs must.

THE JOB

Breeding This is now a controversial subject, with the current bias against surrogate motherhood. But most SDs ignore this and although some breed from necessity — and this is a tiring profession requiring unselfish dedication — some SDs are just delighted when the right chap comes along, they become pregnant and the few extra pennies come in from the puppies as a present for their SDOs.

Writing books Highly acceptable profession for the self-respecting SD with a helpful SDO, and one that can be done in one's own time, which is an added bonus. Amongst others, books have been written by King George V's Sealyham, who wrote *If I Were King George*, and Cefn Mawr McMuck, mentioned earlier, who wrote Debrett's *Top Dog*. Any SD entering the world of publishing is joining an élite group.

Singing Although this doesn't naturally spring to mind as the perfect profession for the SD, there has been a record made of singing dogs, and two SD Wire-haired Dachshunds known to the author — Bertie and Scooter — are always (and only) encouraged to sing every time they hear Rod Stewart's song, 'Sailing'. Thus there are probably several untapped talents awaiting discovery.

71

Showing As with modelling, some SDs do it because they love it and they want to win a present for their SDO, but some do it as a serious living, and these SDs have to work very hard and keep very fit. No late nights, no junk food, and a liking for people and attention is essential.

Modelling Must be prepared to be painted extraordinary colours, get up early and carry around a good wardrobe of accessories, and generally be good at improvisation when required. Being photogenic is a great advantage, but some SDs are happy to be just a catwalk model (though they prefer the term 'dogwalk'). Ideal situation is to be chosen for a long-term advertising campaign.

Acting Great patience, and the same elements of showmanship as required for modelling and showing, are essential. There are some good West End roles (e.g., in *Annie* and *Peg*) which keep an SD with stamina in work for a good few months, or there are film jobs (viz. Benji, Lassie, etc) which are lucrative and can involve travel, but also make heavy training demands. TV is another area of good opportunity — and a long-running television series is a delight to any SD not wanting to tout for work all the time. Be prepared to struggle to the top and work very hard.

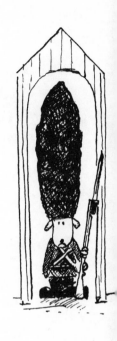

Circus Not a career for making a fortune, really only for earning one's keep. Suits the SD with a sense of adventure who wants to get away from 'family ties', etc. Very 'alternative'.

Guarding A high-risk profession, but for those who are fit, the right size and adventurous, the perfect job, particularly if they can't resist a good fight. Not a particularly Sloane profession unless patrolling in the City, or guarding a bank, a chi-chi estate agent's, or Harrods department store.

Police Very high risk — and certainly not everyone's cup of tea. There will be times when the Sloane Dog's loyalties will be strained — for example, if working in the Drug Squad, or round certain West End clubs on Boat Race night. The

work involves a lot of training and perseverance. An excellent course to take if heroism is your forte, and there are awards such as the Dickin Medal to be won for bravery. These confer great honour on the dog's family as well as giving public recognition of his heroism.

Voluntary work For the SD who doesn't have to earn a living, voluntary work is ideal, and the two major professions in this field are working as a guide dog for the blind or a hearing dog for the deaf.

Guide dogs require patience, understanding and a willingness to make enormous sacrifices. For a start, they are all neutered to prevent their minds from wandering from the job, so have to give up all hope of the patter of tiny paws. They have to devote themselves entirely to their owners, ignoring all the other interesting goings-on in the street, but for those SDs prepared to undertake a life of selfless devotion (and they are few in number) the rewards are tremendous.

The first essential for the hearing dog is that he must be discreet, and very honest, or he can get his deaf associate into all kinds of trouble. Will he repeat all to the *News of the World*? Will he start answering the phone and not passing messages on — manipulating conversations for his own ends? Beware the loud-mouthed SD.

Honorary positions Many SDs are lucky enough in later life to be offered honorary positions as regimental mascots and front-line representatives of entire battalions, an honour shared with the occasional SG (Sloane Goat) and other unusual creatures. These positions are highly enviable and much coveted, as they guarantee a comfortable retirement, good food and warm sleeping quarters.

Part-time work This is the kind of work that can only be done in the season and really comes more into the realm of hobbies, though many country SDs would take exception to that description. Hunting, shooting, fishing — excellent for meeting people, taking exercise and having a good romp. Slighty boring training period. Rather a closed shop — the right breeding is very important. No good if you don't like the taste of bloody feathers.

Then there is that group of SDs who hover on the fringe of work but whose occupations are difficult to define. There is, for example, the Pat Dog, a voluntary worker who visits the sick and elderly and befriends them. Far less honourable is the Lady's Companion, Gentleman's Companion, or indeed the 'kept' SD. The Companions have an easy life and earn their keep by being gentle and ingratiating and relatively lacking in character. They have to be prepared to do clever little party tricks and charm visitors — good for the out-of-work circus dog.

The 'kept' SD belongs to the kept SDO. She is kept as a toy, a pretty and expensive plaything (rather like her owner) and on that basis has to do all the things expected of a mistress's dog, like bark infuriatingly, roll on her back for affection at the worst possible moments, lick faces to wake HIM up at 3 a.m. to go home, and jump up and down with excitement every time she sees HIM.

However much time the Sloane Dog spends on work, though, once work is over, it is time to peruse the social calendar and check out the places to go — in other words, to get down to the real business of Sloane Roverdom.

10 *Where To Be Seen*

If you are a Sloane Rover the world is your oyster, and there are social dates to fix, places to go, and people and dogs to meet. However, it is a sad fact of life that the SD, no matter how Sloane he may be, may encounter the occasional tough time when attempting to go to some of his favourite spots. Not everyone will appreciate his finer qualities. To the uninitiated the SD may be nothing more than a bundle of fleas and faeces. While the SD has long learnt to accept SDOs despite their strange habits and lack of four legs, some humans are not so well adjusted. Thus they sometimes make it difficult for the SD to enjoy all the pleasures of life to which he feels entitled — a glass of pink champagne at the bar in the Connaught, a game of snooker in the Chelsea Arts Club, a luxurious day at the Sanctuary, and so on. It is entirely within the power of the owners of these establishments to curtail these activities if they so wish, and there is no point in creating a fracas (unless one feels like it for fun). After all, one has one's pride to consider.

Bearing in mind the above, though, and apart from the obvious social events that must not be missed, there are restaurants, shops and watering holes that are the right ones to be seen in.

SHOPPING

For the Sloane Dog as well as for his owner the word shopping is synonymous with Harrods. It is a perfect delight to the SD shopper in more ways than one. For small SDs who can fit into a basket it is the ideal place to be carried through, resplendent as it is with luxurious and utterly irresistible items, not to mention the glorious service and wonderful attention one gets. The other overwhelming advantage of Harrods is that the SD who may not feel like being carried round the shop can wait in the dog berths at

76

Door No. 10, which are absolutely perfect for a lie down and a chat to friends. One can meet such frightfully nice SDs in the dog berths, and it is an excellent place to pick up gossip.

Apart from Harrods there are many other shops that one simply has to pop into, or send one's SDO to. Musts include Charbonnel and Walker or Bendicks for one's chocolates, Daks for excellent outerwear, Gucci for superb leatherwear, Butler and Wilson for up-to-the-minute adornment for the Sloane bitch, Paxton and Whitfields for the ultimate after-dinner cheese snacks, Turnbull and Asser for shirts — the collars are perfect — Swaine, Adeney and Brigg for appropriate sporting attire, Liberty's for fabrics — the SDO's dressmaker will be able to create beautiful duvet covers and matching kennel curtains — and, naturally, Asprey's for all those little essentials, from the silver dog bowl downwards. The SD must gradually train the SDO to frequent these haunts.

HAUNTS

There are hotels around the world that SDs frequent, safe in the knowledge that they are in absolutely the right place at the right time, and these are covered extensively in Chapter 12, 'Happy Hols'. Mentioned below are a few London hotels that every SD would enjoy, but we again have to stress that the SDO must phone to reserve and make special arrangements for the SD in order to avoid any unpleasant

scenes in the lobby. There is also a possibility that the small
SD will win over the large SD.

Some suitable SD London hotels

Athenaeum Hotel, Piccadilly

The name alone conjures up English style and charm, which
indeed abound here. Harry's Bar is a must.

Blakes Hotel, Roland Gardens

Every room is individual and exquisite — so don't leave it,
eat in it as well (although the restaurant is very tempting).

Brown's Hotel, Dover Street

The best tea in London — go here instead of Richoux.

Connaught Hotel, Carlos Place

If an SD could choose a place for breakfast — this is it.

Dorchester and Grosvenor House Hotels

Most likely to be seen here after a ball or large party.

And, in the country

Hambleton Hall, Rutland

Fabulous food, Nina Campbell décor, relaxed atmosphere.

Apart from hotels, many SDOs would choose to stay at
'their club'. The SD, however, has less chance of doing this
unless he has left home for good and decided to stay at one
of the RSPCA or National Canine Defence League
establishments — otherwise he has only a few clubs to
choose from. We have already stressed the importance of the
Kennel Club, at 1 Clarges Street, W1, and membership of
this is essential but only possible through excellent breeding.
In addition we recommend the SDO is strongly encouraged
to join the National Dog Owner's Association (39-41 North
Road, Islington, London N7 9DP), which will give expert
advice about anything to do with the SD. Membership also
includes immediate benefits such as third party veterinary
insurance, club events, and newsletters. Moreover, it has
some highly agreeable vice-presidents including Margaret,
Duchess of Argyll and Prince Rainier's sister, Princess
Antoinette of Monaco. Sadly, most gentlemen's clubs will
not open their doors to the SD.

RESTAURANTS

There are restaurants that simply cannot be ignored by serious SDs-around-town and we have listed below a few of the old favourites where one stands a chance of meeting the right sort of associates.

Bistro Vino Cheap, cheerful, comfortable wooden floors.

Peppermint Park Fun, excellent spot to take visiting out-of-towners.

Foxtrot Oscar Spare ribs are good; very jolly; more comfortable floors.

Brasserie Fulham Road Excellent for breakfast, and papers available to read.

L'Escapade Could get squashed underfoot when it gets going — definitely SD.

Draycott's Good spot for cruising — lots of SDOs bring in SDs, particularly on Saturday mornings.

Langan's Say who you are when you book or you might not get a good SD-clocking position, which is most essential.

San Fred's After Draycott's saunter in for Saturday lunch — everyone will be there.

Leonardo's Terrific pasta, great atmosphere, slightly alternative.

Fingal's Named after an SD so a must. Ask to see Fingal — he's delightful.

Café Pelican The length of the restaurant is all the exercise you need for a day.

Café Pacific Food with frisson — go Mexican. Very jolly, but beware the spicy food — don't plan anything indoors for the following day.

As well as places to be seen there is, of course, the social calendar. A mere sketch follows of the highspots of the year, the ultimate SD gatherings.

APRIL

Badminton Dress down, steer clear of jumps with names like Huntsman's Grave and Vicar's Choice. An excellent opportunity to meet the Royal Corgis at last. The Queen sits on top of her Land Rover so you can too. You will probably be so tired from the social day you won't be able to make any of the parties, so take as much champagne as you can from the back of the car. Very much a Husky or Barbour-wearing situation.

Boat Race Not essential, but if you happen to be walking along the banks of the river on the day it's worth a cheer (an excellent excuse to don a light- or dark-blue blazer, and heckle).

Grand National A tiring day, better watched on television with a picnic on the sitting-room floor for atmosphere (Liverpool's not very Sloane, anyway). If fresh air is craved, picnics, radio and binoculars are worth taking along. Be sure to position yourself on a grassy bank near Canal Turn. Wrap up warmly — don't forget the cashmere blanket.

Polo season opens in Durban, should you happen to be there.

MAY

Monaco Grand Prix Only a fixture for the JetSD who has no desire to return to England for six months. Excellent timing for a spot of sun. Stay at the Hermitage or, better still, the Hotel de Paris, where your favourite stool can be reserved from year to year and you can have a view of the exciting bit of the race.

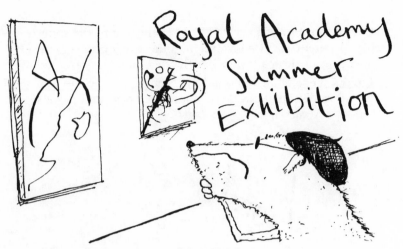

Royal Academy Summer Exhibition Not, frankly, an SD
favourite. Apart from anything else the height of the
paintings gives one neck-ache. Naturally, if you know you
may be in it, then go along.

Chelsea Flower Show This is a very sad event. It is sad
because it is one of those events that has not yet opened its
doors to the canine world and therefore must be missed — it
could be so perfect for the SD as well.

Glyndebourne An excellent SD event due to the superb picnic potential. SDs love picnics and car journeys, but not opera, so in this case they get the best part.

Lord's Test Dull, but good for lapping up the sun and sitting in the open air. Ties should be worn, and jackets, unless it is very hot.

JUNE

Eton — June 4th Excellent fun and a good opportunity to don a boater and watch a procession of boats. Worth going by train and walking over the bridge for a preliminary spot of exercise, and immediate atmosphere.

The Derby If loyal to all the races the Derby is a must — but do make sure you also see the Oaks. Private boxes are fun and some SDs like to go by helicopter.

Royal Ascot Yet another picnic — what bliss! Out comes the cashmere blanket, the *magret de canard* and the champagne. Who bothers about the racing?

Wimbledon Frankly, why bother? Hot dogs are sold in profusion which in itself is enough to put the SD off, and strawberries and cream are not an SD favourite. In addition the grass is forbidden! Watch it on television.

JULY

Henley A dressing-up situation, the joys of boaters and striped jackets. Be sure not to get in the way of irate gentlemen riding their bikes on towpaths — they'll be shouting through a megaphone and are probably coaching something. Hampers abound and to hell with the rowing. Stay up for the fireworks on Saturday night — a good SD was never afraid of a spark or two.

Goodwood Less dress formality and more emphasis on racing which means there is a good mix of SDs and non SDs

Game Fair This requires great discipline and if you think you might get out of control then don't go at all. Location varies annually.

British Open Golf Championship Definite house party situation — out with the tweeds (summer variety) and into fresh lemonade and Pimms. Easier to watch it on television.

Royal Garden Parties Every SD's dream — charitable works is one way to get in. The Corgis, unfortunately, are not in attendance.

Windsor Dog Society Show Championships An SD highlight — and serious chum-meeting exercise. Take the address book.

AUGUST

Polo Ideally suited to fit in with every SD's eating habits as it starts in the afternoon and one can enjoy a civilised lunch beforehand. From Windsor to South America, if you're lucky, it is played everywhere. Watch out for International Polo Day.

Cowes Week Don the life preserver, the soft shoes and the T-shirt, get your temporary membership, then loiter and pose.

Glorious Twelfth At last — the event every SD awaits with baited breath. Revving up begins on the train on the way up to Scotland — much revelry and rowdiness. Frankly, it's a male-orientated event, so excellent if you're a trained SD — but you're likely to get shot if you're not. It is definitely a performance test so skip it if you're out of condition.

SEPTEMBER

Edinburgh Festival Give it a miss — theatre is not the SD's favourite thing and the accommodation is hell enough for the SDOs, let alone the SDs. Fine if you happen to be in a show — lots of social life — but otherwise don't bother.

Burghley Horse Trials Horses again, picnics again, Pimms and pâté, not champagne and strawberries again, beautiful spot again — it's all one continual SD whirl.

Richmond Dog Show Society Championships, Ascot Very SD, very pukka, on no account to be missed.

OCTOBER-JANUARY

Balls Pick your favourite charity (look out for anything connected with National Dog Owners' Association — very SD, very worthwhile), buy your tickets, and dance the night away. SDs might find balls boring as they occasionally end up spending most of the time under the table.

Shooting Now in full swing, try and get on a good variety of shoots and meet so many more chums.

Beaujolais Nouveau A new game, great fun to join the ridiculous SDOs hurling themselves across England (most SDs will only be able to join the race at this side of the water) clutching bottles of red, rather low-key wine. Take a good SD supply of champagne for survival rations.

Skiing Skis are not most SDs' favourite things and though après skiing is fine, the days get so dull and cold. If the SDO goes skiing, suggest you stay behind and house sit.

Scotties' Hogmanay

Boat Show Missable unless keen.

Christmas and New Year What a dilemma — where to be and who to be with? Is it better to be travelling in hot and idyllic spots and forgetting the Yuletide spirit, or sitting by a log fire singing carols? Most SDs go for the family fire, with charades and lots of presents. An ideal time to give vent to eccentricity and dress up in the ultimate SD Santa suit and fill everyone's stockings. New Year, of course, requires the trip to Scotland clutching one's lump of coal and bottle of whisky.

FEBRUARY

Crufts The ultimate SD event, absolutely not to be missed (although at last highlights are now on television, in case of conflicting social events). Only since 1979 has this show been open to women, which is an interesting SDO fact! Worth eyeing up the visitors if foreign travel is your SD aim — exports from Crufts are booming.

MARCH

Cheltenham Horses, mud, marquees — attendance is strictly for the dedicated country SD. For others it's best to watch it on television.

Not all the best places to be seen are in Britain. If one were a very lucky SD one might find oneself in America, and if in America, where better to find oneself than at the White House?

The history of SDs at the White House is excellent, and we have taken some time to mention just a few famous names. Laddie Boy, President Warren Harding's Airedale, sat in a chair and attended cabinet meetings.

President Coolidge and his wife loved all animals and had numerous dogs including Bulldogs (Boston and Beans), two Collies (Bessie and Rob Roy) and a Chow called Tiny Tim.

When Herbert Hoover was trying to improve his image, King Tut, his dog, was wheeled in for photograph sessions with him which won over the public — there are some who say that was how he eventually got in.

President Lyndon B. Johnson had a Beagle called Him who unfortunately got run over but was almost immediately replaced by Yuki, a complete Mélange who won his heart because, according to the President, 'He speaks with a Texas accent — and because he likes me!'

President Nixon was given Ch. King Timahae, an Irish Setter, on his election, and the Kennedy collection of SDs was huge, including Clipper, Charley, Shannon and Wolf — all of different breeds.

In New York, there exists the ultimate tribute to all dogs, Sloane and otherwise, the Dog Museum of America, which is devoted entirely to the study and enjoyment of the dog in art. As well as a great variety of exhibitions mounted regularly in New York, some exhibitions travel to take the Dog all over America. Plans are afoot to expand the facilities, and any support you might happen to give when you are passing will be more than gratefully received.

11 *Playtime*

From puppyhood on the SD will derive enormous pleasure from catching things, ripping them to shreds, and presenting them to the SDO with great pride — and by things we mean everything from dead rats to Charles Jourdan shoes. It therefore becomes obvious very early on that to prevent wilful and manic destruction of all one holds dear, toys and games are essential. Naturally, age will determine the quality and quantity of toys and the style of games — Trivial Pursuits, for example, comes later, particularly the Baby Boom edition. Distraction is what we are aiming for.

The first rule to observe is the removal of shoes from the play area. (Not all shoes — only Charles Jourdan, Bally, Kurt Geiger and Gucci loafers — the SD usually expresses no interest in anything less superior.) Next remove records and valuable furniture. (Don't worry about anything under one hundred years old.)

The obvious immediate solution is The Chew. Sadly, the household chew is an unattractive and uninspiring object and if the SD can be encouraged to use alternatives — say a discarded champagne cork — it will exhibit more style (but make more mess). Don't forget to tell the SD not to eat the cork.

Toys can be divided into three categories: the Up-Front toys — those that friends are allowed to see lying casually around the house; the Park toys — boisterous throwable and visual toys; and finally those No-One-Must-See-This-Disgusting-Object toys which must be kept strictly behind locked doors.

The Up-Front toys include Calvin Klein underwear, the mink cat-shaped toy upon which the SD may vent its fury, the Emanuel-dressed Snoopy dog and the amusing Spitting Image-style squeaky toy — representing a current media personality — these all encourage witty conversation when other SDOs come round for a drink and spot them carefully positioned sticking out from behind a cushion. They are also an indication that you are concerned with the SD's welfare and intellectual stimulation and are making it aware of current trends and preoccupations.

Park toys are a completely different kettle of fish. They include old balls — tennis balls, designer-label golf balls, croquet balls — rubber rings, frisbees and boomerangs (to save the SD retrieving). Golf balls are not recommended for the larger canine as they tend to get swallowed.

Favourite 'for your eyes only' toys differ from the other two categories in that they are almost always chosen by the SD with no help from his owner. They tend to be comforters — the reminders of finest hours, happy families and his favourite armchair — and they are almost without exception pretty disgusting. They are usually such things as dirty socks, massacred and hideous pink plastic hedgehogs that squeak, or whatever item of clothing was thrown on the floor the previous night for washing and instead got adopted and is now the SD's primary comforter.

Aside from toys, it is worthwhile to encourage the SD to take up hobbies. The SD on the whole is not a loner and will be happier to pursue hobbies in conjunction with the SDO, and there are many very suitable ones:

Gardening is an obvious choice, but first check out the SD's natural flair — can he tell a dogrose from a primrose or is he just destined to dig up weeds? Accordingly award your SD a seedbox or a shovel and encourage his development at every possible opportunity.

Amateur surveying — a natural, for the SD can quickly tell how the land lies and enjoys nothing more than an investigative foray. Give him the necessary instruments and a compass for his christening and try to develop his awareness.

Astronomy — many SDs have been awaiting Halley's Comet with bated breath, and as for the eclipse of the moon — this is greeted with positive rapture. Encourage him to sleep on his back staring at the sky and buy a pair of binoculars. The main advantage of this particular hobby is that it keeps the SD awake all night so he should sleep most of the day from sheer exhaustion.

Pot-holing — only feasible if you live in the right sort of area, but a lot of SDs take to this hobby with great enthusiasm and it is often hard to drag them out of the holes. Buy a good helmet and piece of rope as an initial helper then just watch him go.

Keep an eye open for any spontaneous interests developing and immediately encourage them wholeheartedly.

In addition to the obvious amusements like toys and hobbies, there are outings and parties. Party fare has been covered in the Gourmet Guide, Chapter 4, but party games have not, and these can be played at any time provided there are enough chums around to take part.

PARTY GAMES

Pass the parcel

Loosely wrap one Bendicks mint in several sheets of paper fastened with sticky tape or string, sit the SDs in a circle and encourage them to pass the parcel round to music. When the music stops the SD holding the parcel rips off some paper until the music starts again, and the parcel gets passed on. Whoever is holding the parcel when the last piece of paper is removed gets to eat the mint. This is a young SD game.

Hunt the solid gold dog tag

Much more exciting than hide and seek, not to say financially rewarding. Bury the dog tag somewhere clever and tell a group of SDs to hunt it down, giving them very subtle clues at each stage. Whoever finds the tag can keep it and have it engraved with his name. This version is for older SDs, but for younger ones the tag can be replaced with more chocolates.

Poor puss-cat

An SD favourite. One of the SDs has to pretend to be a cat
(tricky sometimes to find volunteers). All the other SDs sit
on the floor and the 'puss-cat' goes round miaouwing and
taunting the individual SDs until one can hold off no longer
and attacks. He is then out. The winner is the one who
manages to prevent himself from being taunted into
aggression.

Give a dog a bone (or a diamond collar)

The choice of bone or diamond collar depends on the age of
the SDs. Put a photograph of a typical SD on the wall,
having written on the back of it the word 'bone' (or
'diamond collar'). Give each competing SD a small arrow
(sticky on one side) and get them in turn to place their
arrows on the photograph where they think the word is
hidden. The SD nearest the target wins. Most older SDs
(except complete gluttons) will crave the collar, while the
younger ones are usually happy with the bone.

Cats and dogs canapé hunt

Resident dogs versus visiting cats — needs some preparation.
Before the game sprinkle canapés both outside and inside the
house, under cushions, under leaves, etc. Invite a local team
of cats (alley cats will add fun as they will be much hungrier
and more determined). Pick team leaders and give them
each a plate. Send the team out to hunt the canapés — the
only ones allowed actually to pick up the canapés are the
leaders with the plates. The team with the most canapés at
the end is the winner. (Eating the booty on the way round
can make for tricky scoring.)

Bonio bobbing

Get large bucket of water and bob Bonios on the surface.
The winner is the one who can get the Bonio out the
quickest without resorting to paws. *Note:* If it takes too long
the Bonio will sink — so don't dawdle.

EXCURSIONS

Excursions are an ideal way of taking an SD's mind off
things as well as being entertaining, thus we recommend
some excursions when the SD has been ill and is
convalescing, as a gentle reviver, as well as a day-to-day way
of passing time.

Picnics These are a favourite excursion. There is no need to
wait for a social event before enjoying a picnic — just dash
into Fortnums, grab a hamper, leap down to the food
department and ask them to cram it full of your favourite
goodies, then rush to your favourite spot (Regent's Park
Rose Garden?) and *mangez. Bon appetit!*

The zoo Pop in on a few friends at the zoo, either in Regent's
Park or make a major epic out of it by trekking further afield to
spots such as Chessington.

River boat trips Take a boat trip up the Thames or along
Regent's Park Canal. Pack a nautical snack and enjoy the
fresh air. (Note for squeamish SDOs — don't pack anything
containing duck.)

Television parties As so many social events are now easier
to see on television, organise a few friends round for
champagne and 'Wimbledon' or 'Golf' or 'Gold Cup Day'.

12 *Happy Hols*

The SDO holiday frequently bears little relation to the SD holiday, and the SD can sniff it in the air. Unless you happen to be going camping in the Fells, fishing in the Lake District or on a walking tour of England, there is a pretty strong possibility that the SD is not about to be invited along. This presents an immediate problem — sulking. As soon as he sees the bags coming out, smells last year's Ambre Solaire and sees the airline ticket slump through the door, he knows it's going to be a lean couple of weeks. In order to avoid this, when making holiday plans for yourself, make holiday plans also for the SD.

If you happen to be holidaying in Britain — not a particularly Sloane habit, but always a possibility — then the problem really does not arise as most hotels will welcome both of you with open arms. It is important to remind the SD of his hotel behaviour and then phone ahead and arrange for the hotel to prepare all or some of the following necessities for the SD guest: any additional blankets that might be required; an extra towel for after his exercise; a

linen napkin (to be changed every day) in the room for the days when he cannot face the crowds in the dining-room; a spare adaptor in case he wants to plug in his heated portable bed (not, of course, in the summer), a radio to listen to and a video to watch.

If you are driving to your chosen British haven, make sure your car is well stocked with games for the SD, as well as travel sickness pills. However well he travels when you pop round the corner to Harrods in the Volvo, it is no reflection of the way he will feel when you hit a forty-mile traffic jam on the M1 in the Easter holidays.

You may well find he will sleep in the car, but just in case it is as well to have a good compilation tape of his favourite songs. This will induce sleep, and along with the occasional energetic burst of 'spot the cat' as you drive through towns, should keep the journey fairly relaxed and uneventful. (Some SDs may find 'spot the cat' too exciting, in which case it will have to be discontinued.) Another good game for the car is putting a favourite morsel into a cardboard Asprey's box with a lid, and seeing if the SD can get into it to eat the goodie. We recommend that this game be encouraged only on the floor in the back, or on the back seat, otherwise the driver's ability to concentrate may be impaired. It is also worth noting that a couple of holes in the top of the box allow the rich smell of chocolate to permeate and encourage more determined playing. (If an Asprey's box is not readily available, any other box will actually do.)

If heading for a good hotel, it is advisable after a five-hour drive to stop slightly before reaching the front door of the establishment to allow the SD to 'take the air'. Otherwise there is a strong possibility he will either damage the entire front lawn, or be forced to disgrace himself upon entering the suite, and before the porters have even left the room.

As well as warning the hotel in advance of what to prepare for their distinguished guest, the SDO must pack a suitcase of favourite possessions as well as essentials, in order to ensure the perfect holiday.

Don't forget the paw wax to protect his pads against the sand and/or the snow. If it is hot, a good-sized spray of Evian water for keeping him cool in the sun is advised, plus, of course, if he will keep it on, a sun hat. Naturally after-sun preparations are a must, as well as anti-peel for the nose. If it's cold then his best coats and wellingtons must be packed. Always pack the tortoiseshell brush and comb set, the Amplex pills and tummy tablets (against the dreaded holiday runs).

Amongst the items that all SDs should travel with is a 'necessaire'. Diana Vreeland used to travel with one she had made to order with a crystal-fitted carafe in which she kept a tot of brandy. In days gone by such things were useful for countering the effects of infrequent trains and sitting in stations for hours at a time — it would seem they should again be introduced.

Providing the SD is consulted daily about the way he would like to spend his time, and he is given a chance to do his favourite things, there should be no problems and the holiday should run like a dream.

The SDO who ventures on a holiday abroad, however, opens up a wholly different ballgame.

The first decision is, are you going to book the SD into a top-class SD hotel, to stay unaccompanied, or is he going to stay with friends — his godparents, for example — while you are away? The choice is actually irrelevant until the SD has been told what is happening.

A highly recommended way of telling the SD of your plans is to take him on an Awayday. Choose his favourite spot — preferably with sun and sea so he can get a taste of the holiday spirit — and spend the whole day chatting things through, walking along the sea front and having a relaxed lunch in a trendy local eatery. Try and arrange the train times so you arrive in good time to find a restaurant for lunch, and so you can also take in a few shops before you head back. Brighton is an excellent spot as it has delightful shops as well as the advantage of the beach, the sea and, of course, a superb pier. Explain the situation in depth and make sure he is happy with the arrangements you are going to make for him, to help him over the trauma.

This exercise is probably not necessary if you are only going away for a long weekend. For this short period friends or dog sitters can pop in just to check his bed is made, he's prepared a good meal for himself, remembered to turn off the television and is keeping up with his exercises. (C.M. McMuck in his book *Top Dog* relays some of the experiences

he has had with dog sitters — one can only conclude that
they must be chosen with great care.)

When choosing holiday accommodation, make sure there
is no limit to the kindness and generosity that will be shown
to him during his stay — his resentment is the last thing you
will need when you get back. Make sure he will have his
own television (sharing is useless if there is conflict over
programmes), video recorder, stereo cassette system, and a
good library of light reading to last the duration.

When the day of departure finally arrives, pack his
suitcase with most of the things recommended for the SD's
stay in a British hotel, but add something of yours to
remember you by — your Husky perhaps? Give him the
telephone number where you are going so he doesn't feel cut
off, and so he knows he can call if his accommodation does
not come up to scratch. Don't forget to take some decent
champagne glasses for his case of champagne, his port, his
Sony Walkman (so he doesn't disturb the other guests late at
night) and a plentiful supply of tapes.

Upon arrival, don't just desert your SD at the door —
take him to his suite, check the facilities, chat to the
manager of the hotel, discuss the restaurant and room
service arrangements, and leave a healthy tip so he gets all
the attention he needs. Then leave quickly and quietly. Bear
in mind that when you return, if he's hated it he might not
speak to you again. Alternatively, if he's loved it he might
not want to leave (SDs can be very difficult).

If the SD is going to stay with friends instead, follow
much the same pattern and take most of the same things.
Explain to the SD that he is very lucky and that if he
misbehaves the friends might not be friends when you come
back. Leave detailed notes on all the SD's little habits —
whether he is a grass or a pavement SD (this can take a long
time to find out), how he likes his eggs in the morning, how
often his washing should be done, what he likes eating most,
and least. (If he's a faddy SD take a good supply of frozen
whatever, otherwise there might well not be any SD to come
back to.) Remember to leave details of his exercise
programme, which gym he goes to, what his favourite radio
and television programmes are. And finally sort out where
exactly he will be sleeping — unquestionably it will be in
the bed. On top of his case pack the photograph of yourself

that you had mounted in a silver frame for the SD's last birthday so he can remember you at your best.

Finally, explain to your friends that they must not pander to the SD — he can be exceptionally difficult. They must not give in if they want to watch the other channel, or have something different for supper. Give them the name of your vet and, of course, the SD's psychiatrist — the latter will be indispensable if he gets determinedly difficult. Also, take a separate bottle of champagne as a thank-you present (apart from the case already delivered for the SD), and a box of chocolates — but make sure they are all centres the SD doesn't like or he will eat them all (coffee creams, violet creams, etc).

One type of SD has not, up to this point, been mentioned — the SD that travels too. This adventurous little devil knows that he will not be able to return to England without staying in quarantine for six months, but he doesn't care. He is the luckiest SD of all, off to see the world and meet his fellow SDs from foreign parts.

Some countries are much more suited to the SD than others. Italy is a favourite spot, particularly as so many Italian artists loved dogs and portrayed them beautifully in their works — the SD loves Italian art. Also many SDs love pizzas! The Italian SDs are a delight to meet because they have such wonderful histories and live in such beautiful estates. They are often hounds and very thin and elegant, unlike the English SDs, although naturally there are a lot of small Yorkies and the odd Labrador as well. English SDs love the family feeling in Italy, and many are also partial to a dribble of Chianti. Ventimiglia market is, of course, an excellent place to acquire some fake Sloanery, and Gucci collars and leads are made in Italy.

France is very popular, particularly the South. A love of French cuisine is not restricted to the SDO; foodie SDs rampage across France with a vengeance in search of delicacies from every area. Nice is a favourite spot for colourful beachery and plenty to do — as they said in *The Boyfriend*: 'It's nicer, much nicer in Nice...'

The poodle rules in France, in all its sizes, closely followed by magnificent larger dogs such as the Saint Bernard or the Pyrenean Mountain Dog. In France the SD enjoys great respect, and it is here that he comes for a wonderful selection of quality leatherwear and accoutrements. The pavement cafés are a source of great delight and enable the SD to stroll happily amongst the French SDOs without feeling in any way uncomfortable. SDs love bidets, unlike some SDOs, because at the end of the day on the beach they can leap in and remove the sand without panicking, as they tend to in the bath, about getting out.

America, of course, is the SD's paradise. Every whim is catered for and no one considers one's eccentricities anything other than very normal. The American SD is very much based on the English SD and they have quite similar tastes, although on the whole Americans have more room both indoors and outdoors and can accommodate the larger SD with very little bother. Many British SDs go to Hollywood to try their luck at becoming a film star — or even just seeing one. American SDs love hamburgers, but know about good beef to put in them. LA SDs have their own health farm called Beverly's Doggerie (mentioned in Chapter 7, 'Excercising Elegantly'), and as American SDs are very star conscious they love places like this where they can rub noses with the SDs of Ryan O'Neal, Zsa Zsa Gabor and Barbra Streisand. Americans are also very pooper-scooper conscious,

which all good British SDs are very keen to promote as they do not like seeing their misdeeds left lying around. British SDs would like to start a similar system here so all the anti-dog lobbyists can see they are not as irresponsible as they are made out to be in the press.

Canada means the great outdoors, lumberjacks, check shirts and canoeing — the ideal spot for the SD with energy. A gloriously clean place and a popular SD holiday spot. Not all establishments are welcoming to the average SD, and Canada is another place not to forget the portable scooper. None the less, every sport is available to the SD with stamina, from fishing to skiing to swimming to bird-watching. An excellent place for the 'get away from it all' week or two. (Canadian SDs are thin on the ground and of varied breeds; analysis would indicate a strong propensity to German Shepherds — Canadians are very butch.) SDs can always apply for a job with the Mounties if they decide they want to stay.

Australia is the place to go for the sailing SD who loves a good cold beer. Sadly we have very few SD reporters down under, but Neddy (named after the much loved Ned Kelly), a first generation English SD of Australian parents, passes on tales of the great outdoors — delicious seafood, glorious steaks, continual barbecues, friendly wombats, aborigines on perpetual walkabouts, cuddly koala bears and hopping kangaroos. His only warning was not to dive into the still waters of the harbour as that is where the sharks are. Neddy himself has not been back to Australia since he left as a mere shrimp, so we are keen to receive other reports from that continent.

Reports of or from SDs in South Africa have been few and far between but we have one SD recently returned from Cape Town who encourages SDs to visit if only for the glorious views and breathtaking beauty of the place. Most of the time the SD will spend by the pool, leaving the SDO to trek into town and socialise. There are terrific open spaces for exercise, and charming people. Kaan, our resident SD, has also recommended some hotels further on in the chapter.

Although India is appropriately Sloane, it is not really a place to which many SDs would want to venture, due primarily to the health risk, and the heat. Indian SDs are thin on the ground.

It would be ridiculous (not to say impractical) to try to cover the whole world, so below are a few international hotel recommendations (only one per country) with the name of the SD who kindly sent in the report:

Paris - L'Hotel Unique and stylish — small and personal. Report sent in by Maurice, an SD Miniature Poodle, who recommends the room lined with leopard skin if it is available when you book (although he points out this may be just a personal fetish).

New York — Plaza Hotel Chuck, whose ancestor Fillet used to work in the gardens at the White House, says the main appeal of this hotel is its proximity to the downtown area. He also recommends the Bel Air in California for their excellent gardens — but says don't forget your pooper scooper. They also have fountains in case you need inspiration — thanks, Chuck!

Montreal — Hotel Bonaventure Scruffy, our SD Wire Fox Terrier, who actually lives in Toronto, always stays at the Bonaventure when he is in Montreal (Scruffy is the derivative of Lord Scruffingdon of Lakeshore). He recommends the open air gardens and pool but also likes the rooms on the inside for their view of the soothing Japanese gardens.

Sydney — Hotel Regent Neddy's parents recommend taking a suite in this well-known Sydney Hotel. They like it primarily for its health club.

Cape Town — Mount Nelson Kaan, our resident Rhodesian Ridgeback of historic parentage, has suggested this colonial-style five-star hotel for its historical feel as well as its fourteen-course dinner menu! Kaan also likes dancing, which the hotel provides every night.

Rome — Hotel d'Inghilterra Mario, an Italian Greyhound with a staggeringly noble background, was thrilled when we asked his advice, and recommended this hotel as it is conveniently close to the Via Condotti and the Spanish Steps. He has, however, been thrown out on occasions, so don't mention his name.

Vienna — Hotel Im Palais Schwarzenberg Fritz, our SD Dachshund on the spot in Vienna, whose great age necessitates the wearing of a monocle, recommends this hotel for its twenty-acre park and the fact that is it owned by Prince Karl Johannes zu Schwarzenberg.

Dachshunds

St. Tropez

Beaulieu — Metropole China's cousins — the Roquebrune Bassets (Max, Totty and Tango) — recommend the tranquillity of Beaulieu rather than the larger South of France resorts, and particularly like the elegance of the Metropole.
In addition we thank the following for their recommendations, though they did not supply details:
Hotel Amstel, Amsterdam — Peder the Bull Terrier
Hotel Pitrizza, Sardinia — Aga the Afghan
Cipriani, Venice — Franco the Yorkie.

All this travelling, however, comes to an abrupt end when the time comes to return to the UK, and SDs must turn their minds to the question of how to manage in quarantine with the massive restrictions it imposes. We suggest a few ways to make quarantine more bearable. The first is to use it, as recommended in our chapter on Education, as a period at a 'finishing' school during which there is time to consolidate all the knowledge gleaned on your travels. There will be a lot of other SDs in the same predicament and they will also want to alleviate their boredom. Many of them will be foreign, and this is the perfect time to trade knowledge — they will be delighted with instruction in what is to be their new language, and you can discuss the habits of their country — food, gesticulations, dress sense, etc — you can even swop recipes. It is also the ideal time to increase the ever-widening social circle, and also to develop an interest in games like bridge, Trivial Pursuits or Monopoly. This will while away many hours and stand you in good stead when you come out.

It is unfortunate that quarantine is the penance for the good time spent abroad, and although it is not ideal, as long as a good arrangement is reached with the SDO to provide regular deliveries of Fortnum and Mason hampers, champagne, cassettes and videos, it can pass relatively quickly and painlessly.

time in quarantine may be used to brush up a foreign language

Sex, Drugs and Rock 'n' Roll

13

The time comes in every young SD's life when the question of passing on the family name and settling down comes to the fore. This marks the end, for a period anyway, of life on the town, revelry and loose living, and the beginning of a new, more responsible attitude.

The young SD will have been nurtured with an eye to the future. SDOs encourage the female SD to make herself as interesting as possible for any suitable chap who might come along; and young studs are primed for action. If a natural choice of partner does not come along, then duty calls and the SD submits to the most suitable chosen partner.

The first stage in what is tantamount to an arranged marriage is the choosing of the partner. Undoubtedly the most correct way of going about this is to get in touch with the Debrett's of the SD world, the Kennel Club, and find the perfect mate to carry on the good family lines. Naturally every SDO would prefer to think that the SD numbered amongst her true and faithful friends at least one suitable suitor, but, of course, this is not always the case. Not all

SDOs think of contacting the Kennel Club and some very unorthodox methods of introduction can ensue. For example, the Lonely Hearts column in various publications is one approach. The advertisement in this case can be tempered to the publication — for the off-beat SD, a *Time Out* advertisement could read as follows:

> Sex-craved bitch, now keen to settle
> down, seeks like-minded stud with
> immediate breeding in mind. Reply
> Box No. 29. Please attach photo.

or for the more discreet:

> Attractive, energetic, well-trained
> male needs intelligent well-travelled
> slim female with view to starting a
> family...

Personal columns in the more serious newspapers are also another possibility, but for these the plea must be more restrained:

> Female companion sought to share
> life of calm serenity and intellectual
> stimulation, and add the essential
> litter...

When replying to these advertisements, the SD should be very wary of signing her or his name — it could be extremely embarrassing if the person who has put the advertisement in the publication is a friend, who might well make it public knowledge that you are 'on the look-out' so to speak.

If you are placing the advertisement it is worth suggesting a discreet initial rendezvous such as the Rose Gardens in Regent's Park, or perhaps by Peter Pan in Kensington Gardens, where you will make a point of wearing the red diamanté collar and lead for recognition.

If the media do not bring success, perhaps the computer — Dateline — is the next possibility. One or two problems arise with the filling in of the form in this case, the main one being height, and many of the questions are really not applicable, so it is probably better to suggest that the SDO insists that all his or her future computer selections have their own SDs. This might be successful, if a little low-brow.

wrong

right

Then, of course, there is the Blind Date. With luck there
will be a jolly kindred spirit who has just found her (or his)
soul-mate who conveniently has a friend in just the same
predicament as you — this way things are kept much more
socially correct. Personal introduction is really what every
SD should prefer.

Although it is possibly unnecessary to point this out, all
young female SDs should be kept in comparative
confinement until the 'moment' is absolutely perfect. Walks
in the park take on a whole new meaning, and the best
investment at this time could well be the jogging machine
to avoid the young female having to flaunt herself in public.
Pamper her, make her feel important, buy her presents —
chocolates, Janet Reger underwear, fluffy slippers —
exaggerate her femininity.

When the appropriate match has been made, the
champagne brought out, documentation checked, 'wins'
discussed and suitability generally analysed, then the matter
can be brought up as dinner party conversation. It is also
the time for the more serious conversation — the
explanations of the facts of life.

SDs, unfortunately, are often very confused about sex. Sex
education is really rather taken for granted — SDOs think
they are supposed to do it like animals, but the animals they
think they are copying often don't have the foggiest notion
of what they are meant to do — or to whom they are meant
to do it. As every SDO knows, some SDs have the
unfortunate habit of performing the most extraordinary
rituals on everything from chair arms to dowager's legs, from
town councillors' coats to children's teddy bears. And this is
not just the male SD — even the female acts in this strange
manner at times, and this performance is even further
removed from what she is supposed to be doing. SDs have
been known to approach cats, rabbits, even gerbils in an
attempt to achieve the impossible. (Rabbits have also been
known to approach dogs — in the ear — but this is a
separate story.)

In addition to this general confusion, there is the question
of which sex the SD should be pursuing. There is not a great
grasp of the difference between brothers, sisters, unrelated
females and unrelated males, and it is at this stage that some
concerned SDOs might wish to seek psychiatric advice. It is

not fair to include this section under 'Sickness and Health' — as it really is more a matter of confusion than sickness — but the SD who wanders in a demented fashion from chair leg to teddy bear and back to chair leg, certainly does need some advice on how to channel his energies in the right direction, as well as full SDO care and understanding.

Naturally not every SD will want to procreate or follow the traditional path, or indeed necessarily be interested in the opposite sex — some will be quite contented sticking to their own sex, and will be proud of it. Some SDs will also have little interest in sex in any form after they have been neutered, and in both the gay SD and the neutered SD the only indication is a predilection for pastel shades and an uncharacteristic lack of interest in rugby.

But back to the impending union. In addition to the 'chat' on sex education it may be useful to leave the odd basic textbook lying around — preferably illustrated and open at the correct page. However, the SDO should make it his or her business to be present at the big moment in case of possible hiccups.

First, set the scene. It is customary for the bitch to stay at home and the stud to visit. Champagne is a must — not so much that sleep overwhelms, but enough to relax the participants. Food is not recommended beyond the odd canapé — it might well result in indigestion or flatulence and that is not helpful. Music is another essential — choose her favourite classical music, light the candles, then pretend you are reading a book and keep an eye out. Suffice it to say that all is going well when the young SDs look like a couple of bookends with smiles all over their faces. However, don't leave yet as they might get stuck and require assistance.

After the event the young SD will remain at the female's house and be entertained royally the following morning with an outstanding breakfast of all his favourite things.

The next few weeks will be tense, waiting to find out if the union was a success. The male SD will keep in touch periodically — it is not done for him to look as if he has loved and left, and if there is no confirmation within a few weeks he might volunteer to drop round with a Predictor kit and offer to settle the matter there and then. Beware the phantom pregnancy — things can be deceptive.

Once pregnant, the Sloane bitch will find her way of life

comparatively boring. Cocktail parties will be curtailed, work will have to be given up, and there will be surprisingly little that she can do comfortably, although popping into the gynaecologist's will provide some amusement, particularly if she has been told she is having twelve sprogs. The odd jumble sale will provide a bit of diversion from pottering around the house and pruning the roses, but the chief source of amusement at this time is likely to come from the ante-natal exercises. Trying to do them will provide hours of hilarity. Maternity wear is not much fun, though some of the fishermen's smocks bought on the last hols in Cornwall may fit, and the diamanté collar, although let out to the last hole, may still go round.

During this last period the SD will need a lot of fuss making of her, and she should be moved into the guest room and made as comfortable as possible. It is a little like looking after the sick or convalescent SD — the television with remote control must be moved in, the pink satin cushions plumped up, the hot water bottles filled (better at this time not to use the cat-shaped ones so she does not get too excited), the enormous box of chocolates purchased, the selection of favourite music carefully made, and, most important, the lightly cooked, nourishing delicacies prepared, full of protein and minerals to nurture the twelve rapidly-growing Sloane infants.

The Sloane bitch and her owner should spend some time during this period musing over the best approach to the birth. Should it be a completely natural one? Ought an

epidural to be considered? Should the puppies be born in the swimming pool (only to be considered if it is a heated, indoor one) or the bath? Is it best to stand, sit or lie down? What music should be played — something stirring like Prokofiev's *Romeo and Juliet*, or something more current, like the Irish Rovers? Should the father be present at the birth? Should it be a home delivery or a hospital one? All these nagging little questions must be answered before the big day. If it is to be a hospital birth the suitcase should be packed ready to leave at a moment's notice, and should include nursing bras (twelve teats can cause problems, and made to measure may be essential), Laura Ashley nightdress and dressing-gown, those favourite pom-pom slippers, a lemon to suck during labour, and a favourite sponge bag brimming over with Floris pungents and potions.

Wherever it is decided that the birth will take place, the moment arrives when the masks go on, the father arrives to hold the paw during the pushing, and the whole drama unfolds, resulting eventually in twelve bouncing little future SDs, all raring to go.

Shortly after she has given birth, the Sloane bitch, if running true to form, will start to turn her attention to the social aspects of early motherhood. As well as learning how to breastfeed twelve boisterous youngsters with discretion in all the best places, her main ambitions will be to work off her excess weight and regain her former figure, and to instil Sloanery in the offspring without delay. To help her lose weight, walks should be upped to at least two a day and the jogging machine brought out from storage for additional aerobics. Traditional exercise patterns can be followed — see Chapter 7, 'Exercising Elegantly'.

Sloanery is harder. Bringing up the young SD is a major role and cannot be taken too lightly; the habits instilled at this young age set the pattern for the future. Ensure, for example, that the newspaper set down for training is only the *FT* or *The Times* — as mentioned earlier, while waiting for inspiration young SDs turn to the news, and they must get it in its proper form. Start now training them to keep their ears out of their food and their elbows off the rim, to say 'lavatory' and not 'toilet', to appreciate the Sloaneness of Peter Rabbit, Winnie the Pooh and Laura Ashley; to learn how to drink out of a silver christening mug; to like jelly and ice-cream, and to appreciate myriads of other essential Sloaneisms.

As the SD gets older, however, there is a new Sloaneism that has to be watched for — and discouraged rather than encouraged — and this is drugs. Watch their Vetzyme intake from an early age and if you see them continually reaching for the jar, and seemingly unable to function without them, then a firm hand is needed. There is no point in fuelling their habit in the hope they will give up themselves, or calling in the RSPCA to give them a taste of the tough life in captivity — they must realize you know, understand, and want to help them. Keep them with you for a period and gradually reduce their Vetzyme intake. The withdrawal symptoms may be unpleasant, but you will have to be strong. Make sure you have cold compresses to mop the fevered brow and if they get very hot, pin up their ears with a clothes peg. See it through, but then, if they still reach for the Vetzymes, you will have to consult the DDAA (Dog Drug Abuse Association) or the RSFSVA (Rescue Society for Sloane Vetzyme Addiction — and they even have a hot line for troubled parents) and take their recommendations.

So, gradually, the youngsters are weaned, the SD mother has instilled the Sloane characteristics, and word is put out on the best SD grapevine that there are several young SDs available to good homes. Some SD mothers who earn their living by surrogacy will already be doing their accounts, and all SDOs should by now be writing out pedigree forms.

The family name has been passed down, and Sloanery continues into a new generation.

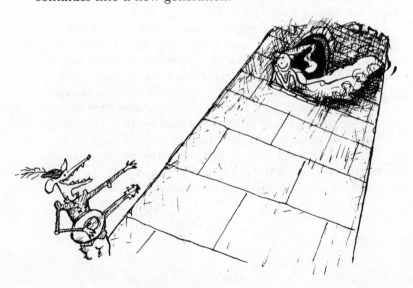

14 *On Show*

The Show SD is the Mr or Miss Universe of the Canine world. It is on him that every pedigree SD models his hairstyle, his ideal physique and his ultimate appearance. From this ideal in each breed the individual takes aspects which he or she can adapt to his or her very own style, but for the Show SD, perfection is the name of the game.

Sadly, the Show SD is frequently misunderstood, and many of the essential nuisances of clipping and shavings are interpreted as mere whims on the part of the judges — people often forget that they go back to the original history of the breeds. The Poodle, for example, because of its traditional trim, is often considered (unjustly) the dumb blonde of the canine world. In fact not only is it an intelligent beast, but the trim was developed owing to the fact that the poodle was employed to round up wounded birds in duck shooting. It was found that its normally heavy coat was a hindrance in water, and consequently was shaved from the end of the ribs down to the tail and on the hind legs. It must be admitted that the tuft on the end of the tail is decorative, but those on the legs are designed to protect the joints from the cold water.

—So there!

Similarly, the Yorkshire Terrier does not merely have bows in its hair as a decoration — it is done to give the dog more freedom of vision while still preserving the smart, silky appearance. The beard and moustache are tied to prevent the dog chewing them away — it is not all frippery.

The Show SD is plucked from the litter at birth and developed with showing in mind. From the earliest days the budding star learns to rely almost totally on natural talent — no flashy nail varnish or coloured contact lenses. Apart from a few useful tips passed on by assorted SD show friends, and listed later in the chapter, there is no outside help allowed.

In the weeks leading up to the show, the SD goes into a period of heavy training. Walkies take on a whole new meaning. Breathing is concentrated on, pace is increased, and working out is a case of really going for the 'burn'. Grooming is constant, the brush and comb never more than the stretch of a paw away, teasing and encouraging the hair in the right direction, getting rid of the fluffy fly-away bits and nurturing the silky bits.

The goal for the perfect weight is set, and the caviare, champagne and Charbonnel and Walkers are put into cold storage until after the show when celebration is inevitable, and feasting quite in order.

Sleep is another must, plenty of it — the eye masks on (two sets essential, one kept in the fridge at all times so the cool mask reduces the puffiness under the eyes) to avoid any distractions. Videos come in useful again at this stage — just before sleeping indulge in some Miss World videos, Mr Universe flashbacks, highlights of last year's Crufts or *Rocky I, II* or *II* videos to heighten the competitive spirit and put hope in the hearts of those who don't think they have a chance.

As the time passes the SD begins to think about the smaller details. What is the SDO to wear to show him off to the best advantage? (Nothing too showy — perhaps subtly coordinating with the SD's collar and lead.) Which bag is the SDO taking for carrying the essentials in? Will it, too, coordinate? It is stressed again by some old hands that restraint is the order of the day. Do not include anything remotely contentious — no hair colour, no overtly flashy solid gold collars or silver dog bowls, no false eyelashes, or

cosmetic toothpaste — nothing with which to make the other contestants jealous. The budding champion needs all the support he can get, so there is no point in antagonising the competition.

Crufts is the crème de la crème of the dog shows, and no SD gets there without a great deal of dedication and determination. There are classes at many more humble shows that have to be won first. The Show SD must prepare himself for a round of exhibitionism if the Best of Show at Crufts is the ultimate goal.

There is a standard procedure for all shows that must be learnt, and we outline below a typical show day, with some of the pitfalls and some of the essentials.

Before leaving home, the SD should check that the SDO has the exhibitor's pass with him — without this he cannot get in. Equally, however, without its being signed and handed in upon leaving, the SD cannot be dragged out by some thieving maniac trying to pick up a free dog.

SDs should also be prepared for a veterinary examination before going into the show, to avoid some of the current nasty diseases being spread far and wide (almost, but not quite, the canine equivalents of herpes or AIDS). The SD will then have a number allocated to him which is his bench number and the SD and the SDO will go to this bench immediately. Some SDs might fall off the bench in a fit of nerves, so do keep an eye on them. Disinfect your bench, just in case, then lay out your rug (discretion determines whether you have dared bring the £600 cashmere or not — it might well go against you).

Next find a catalogue of events and note what time you go in — it would be foolish to miss your event.

Don't forget, if you are a novice show SDO, to let your SD go for a 'stroll' before the event — you would hate him to have to walk round with his legs crossed.

If you forget any of the SD's essentials, don't panic, there are always suppliers at the shows who will be delighted to sell you whatever you need.

If you win, don't go screaming around waving an invoice for the prize money. Casually stroll to the Treasurer's office to collect it.

The actual showing procedure is rather technical and may be beyond the grasp of the average SDO. Suffice it to say that the owner walks the SD round the ring (with the dog between him or her and the judge), and at the time of passing the judge, mutters some favourite words such as 'Caviare!' or 'Siamese cats!' to make the SD look animated. After parading round for a while the dogs and owners will come to a halt, and here the SDO has to ensure that his SD adopts the right posture for his or her particular breed. For example, a Dachshund may be encouraged to stand with one hind leg stretched out behind so the line of his back does not appear to go upwards at his rump; a Labrador should stand four-square and firmly, as befits his *persona*; a Springer Spaniel should look natural. Such is the Cavalier King Charles's disinclination to exertion that it is difficult to get him to stand at all, as he much prefers sitting.

If you have far to drive before a show, try to avoid doing it on the day of the show itself — if it is Crufts, for example, come up to London and book into a suite at a top hotel the day before. This is partly because the nervous SD will probably not travel well despite Chloreton tablets for car sickness, or even phenobarbitone against hysteria, and thus will not look his best for his major moment. The other advantage of the suite in a good hotel is that it makes an excellent venue for the press to return to and be entertained at, and for the champagne to be drunk out of the champion cup.

Some generous show SDs have given us a few tips, and we are happy to pass these on to any young hopefuls:

- On the day of the show, nails should be polished or touched with cotton wool on which there is a trace of brilliantine.

- The dry silk scarf rubbed over the coat gives a wonderful sheen.

- Chalk can be used for whitening the coat provided it is well brushed through.

- Character is as important as looks — don't think you can get away with being pretty and very dumb — cringing and flirting will get you nowhere even if you are outstanding to look at.

- Practise your poses the day before the show, including how to smile for the cameras in case you win. Work out the best and worst profiles. Make it all second nature so you don't panic.

- Check the names of the judges before the event, you might have met some of them before, and it can't do any harm if you recognise them.

The SD will probably know most of these tips already, and, of course, while lounging nonchalantly on the bench on the blanket, cleaning his teeth with his toothpick, he will also be keeping an eye out for visiting dignitaries and famous faces. Occasionally royalty makes its presence felt, and if not English royalty, Princess Antoinette of Monaco is sometimes seen and is a delight to chat to.

And so the tension mounts, the big moment arrives — the SD leaves the benches, the heats begin. Chewing on an Amplex tablet and smelling faintly of Harrods new perfume Eau de Toilette Prima (£9.50 a bottle in the pet department — a modest flash gesture and not to be overdone or the judges might disqualify you), the SD strolls casually over to the ring. He smells delicious, is breathing spring afternoons, is brushed, silked and gleaming, his answers ready for the judges in order to shine in the personality-testing questions (ambitions — to start a guide dog for the blind school, favourite hobby — retrieving birds from large lakes, one wish — to win Best of Show). The rest is luck.

15 *In Sickness And In Health*

The SD and the human baby have one thing in common when it comes to being sick — their inability to communicate exactly what is the problem. However, although backward in coming forward on the exact nature of the illness, it is guaranteed that the SD will maximise the severity of it and enjoy enormously the fuss potential. Meanwhile, the SDO is probably tearing his hair out worrying about the cost potential — but never fear, Pet Plan (35 Horn Lane, W3), the BUPA of the canine world, is at hand. Contact them immediately and join, to be on the safe side.

There are two common illnesses that require only cursory mention and even more cursory sympathy — the results of over-eating, and a hangover. Both manifest themselves in much the same way as the SDO's over-indulgence, and require similar treatment. Over-eating results in flatulence, sickness and a continual desire to tread the great outdoors; hangovers in red eyes, wobbly knees, sickness and

overwhelming self-pity. For the former, starvation, a glass of Andrews, and straight to bed is the answer. For the latter, a cool pack for the forehead, Andrews and an early morning filler of bacon and cheese toasted sandwich (or personal favourite) and a good hangover cure. The Hair of the Dog is particularly apt and the recipe is mentioned in Chapter 4, 'Gourmet Guide' (see page 43).

If, however, the SD is showing signs of serious illness, the vet has to be called, a state of emergency proclaimed and a mammoth programme of fuss and attention put in motion. The spare room will come into its own, for the SDO will have to explain to the reluctant SD that he cannot sleep in his owner's bed when he has... (whatever infectious disease it may be). An electric blanket must be put on the bed, the portable television, video, Sony Walkman and a supply of cassettes, videos and video games placed to hand, some favourite Benji films must be made available, and a large bell provided should the SDO's assistance be required. Pink satin cushions will comfort the ailing female SD and the warmth of the colour will flatter her pallid countenance and make her feel cherished.

The medicines required will naturally vary according to the illness, but there are some good standbys which constitute sick-room fare and should supplement the potions and pills that might have been prescribed. Warm Marmite laced with a dash of good malt whisky before sleeping is an excellent knock-out drink. Brand's Essence in a variety of flavours is popular, or just a good consommé — perhaps chicken with fresh chicken pieces added for substance. Baby food may well be necessary, or alternatively, as most SDOs have a Magimix these days, simply blend whatever one had for one's own meal — or if you have been out for dinner (how could you with a sick SD upstairs in bed?), then blend the contents of the doggy bag. Naturally, hand feeding may be necessary to revive the flagging appetite.

The range of illnesses SDs are prone to is vast and varied. Muscular strain is quite common when the perky SD over-extends himself. Many SDs have disc problems (a particularly OK SD complaint), and as with SDOs these problems are very hard to pinpoint and cure. Physiotherapy is the first suggestion, and this will require the assistance of the SDO with some of the tricky positions that the SD will

be forced to assume to try to cure the problem. Note the
need, with back problems, for low beds and floor-height
tables, etc.

Massage is a form of physiotherapy popular with SDs and
can help many different kinds of illnesses. Naturally we are
not referring to the unsavoury Soho massage parlour (and if
any wayward SD is seen clinging on to his tube season ticket
and heading for Oxford Circus or Tottenham Court Road,
waving his walking stick with enthusiasm, he should
immediately be diverted with a few strong words).

Some SDs such as greyhounds and other professional
athletes will find the period surrounding muscular injury
particularly hard to endure as training is all-important in
maintaining their success on the track. SDOs should be very
patient and understanding but also very firm, and make sure
they do not try and get out of bed or leave the house.
Perhaps a continual supply of blue movies might be a way
to keep him occupied, or if his mind does not incline that
direction, then a Berlitz course in a new language.

injured
Greyhound

Aside, of course, from purely physical illnesses there are more complicated problems of a psychiatric nature, such as stress and emotional trauma, and for these there is always the reassurance of the animal psychiatrist.

Stress can be caused by many things: noise, emotional upheaval (moving house, a death in the family, pregnancy), or the effects of a traumatic upbringing. The Duchess of Argyll's dog, Alphonse, was recently forced to leave an SD fashion show due to the noise level which he found far too upsetting. There is also stress caused by frustration — not being able to catch the cat next door, or get at the bitch next door — or perhaps the SDOs are arguing a lot and this is having an effect on the SD. This could require an immediate holiday — either the SD or the SDO should go away for a week on a health farm and pamper themselves out of the problem. Or the SD should visit his club in St James's and spend a few days away from the hubbub of family life, in the bosom of genteel respectability.

If a holiday is not possible, then immediate alternatives should be considered. Yoga is one suggestion. It has been recommended before, for aiding with training, and in this case also it is particularly suitable. Hydrotherapy is another good alternative. A jaunt to the RAC club (male SDs only unless wives or daughters under thirty) with a qualified therapist and a few energetic hours spent working on the problem is really very therapeutic.

Faith healing or radiesthesia (a form of psychic healing) are currently in vogue and have proved particularly effective on racehorses. In fact the current enthusiasm for alternative veterinary medicine makes it well worth considering. (Even the Prince of Wales considers it.) According to the ailment there is a homeopathic medicine, chiropractic and acupuncture. Psychotherapy — just talking to the SD — is also often a great help. The SD may well find these alternatives not only more successful, but also much more interesting, than conventional medicine, as well as making excellent dinner party and gentlemen's club conversation topics after the event.

Convalescence is often harder for the SD to endure than the illness itself. Though feeling better he will not be allowed to rush about in his usual manner, and the SDO will have to come up with lots of imaginative ideas to keep him relaxed and interested.

physiotherapy

acupuncture

hypnosis

osteopathy

Convalescence

All the boredom deterrents will have to be dragged out —
the cards for endless bridge rubbers (two friends will have to
be willing to help here), or for Snap in severe circumstances,
the Tom and Jerry jigsaws, old movies for the video, even
risqué paperbacks like *101 Uses for a Dead Cat* — anything to
keep his pecker up. Occupational therapy could be given a
whirl, for example, basket-making, needlework, painting, to
revive lost talents. A darts board can be set up in the
bedroom with a picture of his arch enemy, or rival in love,
for the bullseye. Chocolates can be hidden around the house
and chocolate hunts set up to keep him indoors. If he is well
enought to go out, organise a few day trips. He might enjoy
a trip to the dog track to see some chums chasing the odd
hare (though this is slightly cruel as it will undoubtedly
revive his own interest), or a day shopping in Knightsbridge,
buying cakes from Richoux on the way home and eating
them as soon as you get in. Or perhaps a day on the river.
Drive down to Oxford in the Bentley Continental, rent a
punt and pole the SD gently downstream, with, of course, a
picnic hamper on board, the champagne cooling in the crab
pot under water and Mozart playing on the Walkman —
perfection. (Note: this must only be done in midsummer on
a sunny day, it is not recommended for December or in the
rain.)

If the illness is of a more permanent nature, then the SDO will have to be very careful not to offend his dog's sensibilities. One of the most unfortunate things that can happen is paralysis of the back legs, which can be caused by disc trouble, amongst other things. A solution to this problem has been found which involves attaching a permanent scooter to the back portion of the SD, enabling him to 'walk' as well as, or even faster than, before. We felt this was worth mentioning in case SDs should bump into someone with this problem at a cocktail party and think it was a hooray SD joke, which could be very embarassing. Comments like 'Can you give me a lift home?' or 'Is there room for two on that thing?', would not go down particularly well.

One misfortune which befalls the SD as often as the SDO, is the hunting accident. The chase is on, the pack are in top form, the speed increases and wham! down a rabbit hole the poor hound goes — and his leg is a goner. Naturally nothing stops at this stage, so the hound must realise he should stay where he is and relax until someone is sent to find him. He will feel humiliated — show him sympathy. When he is lying, his leg in plaster winched high above his bed, next to his friend who ran across a rugby pitch in the middle (literally) of a ferocious tackle, don't laugh — take him

grapes and exude calm understanding. Cheer him on, tell him the pack is missing him, don't chastise him, he is a sensitive beast.

Naturally, in day-to-day life, just like the SDO, the SD can suffer many strange, inexplicable maladies, some of which may remain with them all their lives but give little trouble. King George V's Sealyham, Jack, developed the curious practice of fainting with pleasure when he saw familiar faces. On the last occasion he saw his master, in 1928, it is reputed that he fainted three times!

16 *Unfortunate Unmentionables*

The overwhelming regret of all SD owners, and indeed most
SDs themselves, is that they cannot use the loo. It would
make life so much easier all round. SDOs learn to tolerate
this fact, but the SD feels very aware that no one has yet
bothered to come up with a suitable design (as they have for
cats) that would make this possible. There is an unsavoury
object called a dog loo that is extremely useful, but can only
be used in the garden and it is not a direct receptacle, it
requires scooping and depositing.

Every SDO's dream is to cultivate the SD who only wants
to go once a day under cover of night. This is unrealistic.
One of the major things that puts non-SD lovers off SDs is
that they excrete where non-SDOs want to walk. It must be
the responsibility of the SDO to ensure that this doesn't
happen in order to avoid the SD becoming a target for over-
anxious mothers and anti-SD campaigners. There is an
organisation called Pro Dogs (4 New Road, Ditton,
Maidstone) set up expressly to promote responsible dog

127

ownership, which will be glad to answer the SDO's questions about the way to behave with his or her SD. In New York it is now commonplace for people to make a citizen's arrest if they see anyone allowing the SD to foul in the wrong place and not poop-scooping afterwards, and although the UK SDO may mock this idea, can he suggest an alternative? Even in Paris, a company has been formed by the name of Trottoir Net (which means 'clean pavement') to clean up after dogs. Using a fleet of Yamaha XT 240 motorcycles bearing rotary brushes and storage containers, the eighty green-suited operatives of Trottoir Net cover 1,000 miles of Paris pavements a day. At the end of the day up to one and a half tons of the 'refuse' is collected, sealed in biodegradable bags and thrown into the sewer. Excellent news.

The mainstay of the cleaner canine campaign is, of course, the Poop Scoop. In America there is a choice of Scoop from shovel type with long handles to bulldog-clip-bend-down-and-get-it design, to a fishing rod-type with garbage bag at the end. In Britain, however, there is not such a good selection. One cannot pretend that the British Poop Scoop is easy to drop into a handbag, or that it is particularly attractive, but it is very useful. The market is open for the disposable handbag model.

The next nagging question is — where does the SD do it? Apart from parks which are unavoidable targets (although some do have their own dog 'loos' in the form of sandpits with encouraging notices) there are several serious no-nos, some of which, if in the proximity of a warning notice, carry a maximum fine of £50:

- Not in the dog bays at Harrods.

- Not outside the entrance to Harrods, Nieman Marcus (you'd be arrested there anyway), Harvey Nichols, the General Trading Company, Peter Jones, Osborne and Little, or, with slightly less emphasis, any shop or on any main streets, particularly in Knightsbridge, Sloane Square (sacred ground), etc.

- Not on people's doorsteps, even if they are not Sloane.

- Not right by the door of a stationary car.

- Not on buses or tubes or any form of public transport — primarily because it's extremely embarrassing.

- Not in taxis.

- Not on aeroplanes.

- Not on the QE2.

So where? The element of embarrassment experienced by the SDO means that it will undoubtedly be somewhere discreet, but complaints will still arise if the discreet spots chosen are somebody else's favourite begonia patch.

Some favoured discreet(ish) spots include:

Mews Unfortunately for those who live in them, the SD tends to like mews because they have often got cobbles which seems to satisfy the SD who cannot get used to pavements.

The gutter This is the commonly accepted spot, it incurs little wrath and is relatively discreet, but be careful it is not right by someone's car door.

Front lawns This is unfortunate, particularly for those who do not have an eight-foot-high wall around the front of theirs. They are an immediate target for the SD who hates the pavement and most SDs do seem to prefer grass. (It is advisable for the SDO to walk swiftly on past at this choice of spot and wait for the SD just around a nearby corner.)

Building sites When the builder is not watching.

It is hard to give advice as to what the SDO should do if the SD disgraces himself in a particularly unfortunate public place — the most sensible but highly unsporting suggestion is to move like greased lightning and remove yourself from the vicinity as fast as possible, apologising as you run.

Pooping is not the only problem that SDs have. Peeing on carpets is another. Luckily SDs often grow out of it, but sometimes only to grow back into it when they become old and incontinent. There are several remedies going by such names as Stain Off, or Not a Mark, or even strong-smelling deterrents which put the SD off the whole idea in that particular spot. Indeed there is now even a magical carpet available from the Ollerton Hall Decorating Service (Ollerton, Knutsford, Cheshire) which is considered pee-proof and guaranteed for seven years. Buckingham Palace is reported still to resort to the soda syphon, and to have them

dotted liberally around the palace in case of emergency. There is no higher authority than that.

Biting the postman is another nasty habit that the SD might pick up, which brings to mind the words of a verse by Oliver Goldsmith:

> The dog, to gain some private ends,
> Went mad and bit the man,
> The man recovered of the bite,
> The dog it was that died.

Although biting is well meant and an attempt at guarding the house, the SD must be taught that the friendly postman is performing a necessary public service. On these occasions immediate action should be taken. Appease the postman with a large whisky (or suitable alternative), soothing words, and possibly iodine and a large plaster. Wash the dog's mouth out immediately with a good antiseptic mouthwash and rush out and buy him a copy of *Postman Pat* so that he gets the picture more clearly.

Sexual mania has already been covered generally under 'Sex, Drugs and Rock 'n' Roll' (see Chapter 13), but it can often form rather an unfortunate and persistent habit. Unfortunately some SDs firmly believe that every object of approximately the right shape and size is there for the sole purpose of sexual release, be they male, female, animal, vegetable or mineral. It is absolutely fine if this is a passing phase, or if it is related to a bitch on heat in the vicinity, but when it is a compulsive and continual habit which results in broken furniture and mauled upholstery, not to mention ravaged visitors, the problem has to be tackled. Neutering is often the only solution and will put an end to the manic Hooray Henry approach to life that has driven the household to despair. This will undoubtedly result in feelings of deep resentment on the part of the SD, and there will be a difficult period while the SD comes to terms with his lack of virility. It is at this point that he might also change dramatically, possibly even taking up cooking or interior designing, and rejecting the old favourite sports like rugby and hang gliding.

Drunkenness and theft are two more dramatic habits that might get out of hand. It may well be necessary to mark the bottles and keep an eye on the mixers if the SD is keen on spirits. Champagne will be much harder to tell, particularly if the SDO has an enormous cellar — the occasional bottle from the back will never be noticed. When you discover the problem, treat it firmly but kindly. Make the SD face up to it, then try and encourage him along to AAA — Alcoholic Animals Anonymous — where he will make some good friends and get the support he needs. Lock the cellar and make sure he is watched subtly but carefully when he is at Ascot or Badminton. Keep the boot of the car locked when the picnic is over so he can't nip in and finish the supplies. Stop taking him to so many cocktail parties. In other words, remove the temptation. Stealing is usually a product of bad education. Whereas drinking might well be related to some emotional trauma, stealing is usually wilfully mischievous. It usually only relates to food, so the main inconvenience is putting locks on the fridge and the pantry. If it extends to personal possessions and money, it is definitely time to refer the SD to a counsellor for delinquents. (Check the stealing is not just chewing, in which case the evidence will be revealed on the evening round.)

Chewing is a tricky problem, again one that usually improves as the SD gets older, but in the destructive first year car interiors as well as house interiors have been known to suffer the ravages of infant teeth. In this case the SD must be given all the chewing material he can handle as an alternative to the things he is not allowed to chew — neither

don't fuss darling — he's so much more sensitive now

of you should leave the house without filling all your pockets with enough chews to distract him from the Louis XIV chair legs upon arrival at another glorious SDO home.

Aggression and wilful violence is another unfortunate SD problem area, more prevalent in small, short-legged dogs. Guests can be deprived of a section of their socks at a moment's notice, and trousers frequently suffer badly. Discipline is all-important, and may need to be supplemented with psychiatric advice and understanding rather than brute force. Try to understand the reason for the violent outbursts, and encourage the SD to take up boxing. Better that he vents his fury on a punch bag rather than people.

17 *Last Post*

THE WRINKLIES

Old age is not really a whole heap of fun. The average SD is a wrinkly at the age of eight or nine and it is then that the ravages of his decadent life begin to take their toll. The oldest recorded dog lived to the age of twenty-nine, and perhaps there should be a letter from the Queen if dogs reach the age of fifteen or over.

Like the SDO, the SD is continually searching for the secret of eternal life, and is happy for any tips he or she can pick up along life's happy path that might lead to living longer. As the years creep on and the devotion between SD and SDO gets greater, departure on either side becomes a very traumatic experience. There is no evidence to confirm whether champagne, Charbonnel and Walkers and caviare increase or decrease the chances of longevity, but it is undeniable that they are highly enjoyable, and would be sorely missed if proved detrimental.

The physical aspects of old age are not much fun, and the deterioration has to be taken like a trooper and coped with as well as possible. The teeth are one of the first things to go and false teeth are not always practical. The best advice one can give is clean regularly and don't forget the dental floss. Hair is not such a problem. Thanks to Grecian 2000 those grey hairs can quickly be disguised, the giveaway areas around the SD's ever-dignified muzzle can be restored to normality and no one need ever be able to place an age on him again.

As a young SD — particularly if you are a working SD — it is worth considering taking out an insurance policy so the next of kin can be properly cared for when you are dead and gone. If there are no next of kin, the nest egg could perhaps pass to the SDO who has nurtured you all this time. Consult the National Dog Owners' Association for all matters of this kind, they will be only too happy to give sound advice. Alternatively go direct to THE pet insurers, Pet Plan, as mentioned earlier.

If deterrents have not worked, youth slips away and illness creeps up with old age, the wrinkly SD must consider some of the treatments available to make his last years more comfortable.

Physiotherapy and massage are excellent not only for the sick SD as mentioned before, but also as a revitalising treatment for depressed old age. It is amazing how the sight of a young physiotherapist can revive a flagging wrinkly and remind it of better days. Definitely worth the extortionate fees (only private will do — after all, it is the SD's last years), and certainly worth the large amounts of time on the part of the SDO that this treatment will involve.

Alternative medicine is particularly attractive once the SD has reached this stage, and even though in his younger days he may have pooh-poohed the offbeat treatments available, it is now that he may realise their value. If the SD suddenly disappears and is nowhere to be found around the house, there is a strong possibility he is trying meditation in the loft, zen buddhism in the garden shed, acupuncture in Harley Street or foot/paw feeling (reflexology) in Holland Park. The yearning for lost youth may well go to his head, and senility can begin to be a problem.

Senility takes many forms. The SD might regress and go careering around the garden chasing butterflies, only to come to a wrinkly realisation and a dislocated hip halfway round the grounds, and have to be carried in for a period of remedial treatment. Alternatively the SD might start believing he is once again the Crufts champion he was, start trying to work out and build up to a come back, drag the satin boxer shorts out of the loft and book an appointment with the poodle parlour (let him keep this). He might just become absent-minded, forgetting to put his collar on in the mornings, losing the way to the kitchen, not remembering to wash his hair regularly, the only solution to which is a gentle reminder.

Although back problems are often prevalent throughout the SD's life, they can get infinitely worse in his old age, and one solution to this may be the surgical corset. It may look a little strange, (it can, of course, be disguised under a jogging suit, which is now a much toned-down item of the wardrobe, in keeping with the SD's dignified age), but this corset, combined with good support hose, can be the answer to the gradually collapsing figure.

In the final months of the SD's life, try to cheer him up by taking him back to some of his favourite haunts to say his last goodbyes to some of his friends. (This might be delicate

last look at Harrods

if incontinence is a major problem, and might only be possible after a long session at the acupuncturist, or the foot feeler.) Pop into Annabel's or Raffles for a late night drink, lunch one last Saturday at San Freds, pop into Harrods for a last wander through the pet department. Let the SD experience a final stroll in his favourite parks — in short, consider all the things *you* would like to do at this stage in *your* life — after all your turn will come, and the SD will be waiting for you in that Sloane House in the sky.

There is always the issue of 'should the wrinkly SD go into a home' but it does not even bear reviewing.

THE PARTY'S OVER

When the wrinkly SD feels it is finally time to say goodbye, he will call the family to his side in the master bedroom, which he has had to occupy for the last six months or so due to illness (his owner won't have minded sleeping on the camp bed, it was the least he could do), and hand over his will, which he will have kept buried in a suitable spot and authorised his young nephew to dig up.

At this time the SDO will have to be very strong and steel himself to do the right things. The priest will have to be called and the last rites administered (some SDOs might have to leave the room at this stage due to overwhelming emotion), or the SD may call for a last toast with champagne all round, or a final Charbonnel and Walker (only soft centres, now, due to lack of teeth), and raise his glass to 'the good life' — his final gesture.

Firstly — Get a Grip. Although SDOs are normally quite low key about the demise of one of their number, when it is the SD's turn it is quite a different matter. If getting a grip is quite beyond you, it is acceptable to consider taxidermy and arrange for the honourable SD to be stuffed for posterity and keep his place by the fire for all eternity. But if getting a grip is possible, it is preferable. Some SDs might even insist on taxidermy themselves, but try and dissuade them if you, the SDO, are not keen on the idea.

Once the grip has been got, the will can be read. To whom has the silver bowl been bequeathed? What are the death duties likely to be? (Some shrewd SDs will have arranged for all monies to be transferred prior to their death to avoid this problem.) Is it to be burial or cremation? These matters should all have been outlined in the will, along with who will inherit the large wardrobe of clothes and the brass bedstead.

Many people prefer a private funeral, with the SD buried in a lavish coffin on home territory at the bottom of the garden, and the grave marked by a quality remembrance stone. Cremation is the alternative, though some SDOs find

this all too upsetting, so rather than a social gathering at the time they prefer to opt for a memorial service and cocktail party at home a week or two later. For detailed information, again contact the National Dog Owners' Association, or ask the vet, who will be only too happy to make his recommendations.

If the SDO is lucky enough to have a family vault, in some cases it may be possible to arrange for the SD to be buried in it also. If not, it is possible to have his effigy added to those of the family buried in the tomb. Queen Alexandra arranged for Edward VII's favourite dog, Caesar, to follow the gun-carriage carrying his coffin during the funeral procession, and four years after Caesar died she added his effigy at the base of his master's tomb in St George's Chapel, Windsor.

In America, the SD funeral is treated with enormous pomp and ceremony and lavish coffins are designed for departed SDs. In Britain and Europe, however, this does not seem to be quite so popular.

Both for home burial and for the pet cemetery, the headstone is an important consideration. Unless a very ornate headstone is required (angel of mercy standing over the grave, lifesize statue of the deceased in bronze guarding the plot, etc.) a simple stone with a fitting epitaph is recommended with a good but not ostentatious coffin in the grave.

Some favourite epitaphs are listed below as a guideline:

'Of puppies in all she bore
    twenty-four
Thank the Lord there will be no more.'
         from Canterbury, Kent.

'Charity, dog of Gideon Bligh,
Underneath this stone doth lie,
Nought was she e'er known to do
That her master told her to.'

'Be comforted, little dog, and know that
   at the Resurrection
you too shall have a golden tail.'

'Here lies the bones
of Phideaux Jones
Who ate while he was able.
But once o'er fed
He dropt down dead
And fell beneath the table.
When from the tomb
To meet his doom
He rises amid sinners,
Since he must dwell
In heav'n or hell
Take him — which gives best dinners.'

Easily adapted possibilities

'Oh great Sloane Dog
How could you go?
At Crufts next year
We'll miss you so.'

'Oh Noble Grub,
You fearless beast,
You could have waited
For me at least.'

Serious

'Alone of Gods Death has no love for gifts,
Libation help you not, nor sacrifice,
He has no altar and hears no hymns,
From him alone Persuasion stands apart.'

Aeschylus, *Niobe*, tr. C.M. Bowra

'They say, God wot!
She died upon the spot,
But then in spots she was so rich —
I wonder which?'

Thomas Hood,
'On the Death of a Giraffe'

Lengthy

'Though once a puppy, and though Fop by name,
Here moulders one, whose bones some honour
    claim;
No sycophant, although of Spaniel race!
And though no hound, a martyr to the chase!
Ye squirrels, rabbits, leverets, rejoice!
Your haunts no longer echo to his voice
This record of his fate exulting view —
He died worn out with vain pursuit of you.
"Yes!" the indignant shade of Fop replies,
"And worn with vain pursuit, man also dies".'

William Cowper,
'Epitaph on Fop'

The end